cocina nueva

the new spanish kitchen

Jane Lawson

MURDOCH BOOKS

contents

Synonymous with Spain, tapas bars, known as *tascas*, are
'the' venue to start or end an evening. Whet your appetite
with a tantalizing small plate accompanied by an aperitif
of fino sherry, or spend hours sampling the delicious
specialties of the house over a few glasses of red.

The heart of the home! 'Cocina' means both kitchen
and cooking in Spanish. Food from the Spanish kitchen is
flavoured with passion and love. It is all about comforting
and hearty meals that utilize the best of local produce, be
it slowly simmered or quickly seared.

Traditional desserts are simple and luscious — whether
it's silken custard, a slice of *turron* or a sample of juicy ripe
fruit. Contemporary recipes showcase the sweet flavours of
Spain — irresistible offerings of chocolate, coffee, citrus and
toasted nuts mingled with exotic spices, from warmly
scented cinnamon to heady saffron.

introduction

My first trip to sunny Spain was a whirlwind trek through dusty plains, whitewashed coastal enclaves and clifftop villages in what became a quest to tick off some imaginary checklist of Spanish icons, from greying donkeys to the windmills of La Mancha. Sadly, I was barely able to get a whiff of any culinary scene, our exhaustingly disinterested guide assuring me in her Cockney accent that Spaniards 'only ate pork or fish', and that the dried-up, teeth-breaking portions we were attempting to consume were completely typical. Knowing this was a complete load of *el toro* I vowed to return.

And return I did, my most recent trip providing an enticing insight into the new and sexy, sophisticated Spain of today. Being a 'foodie', my travels are predominantly cuisine inspired, seeking out restaurants, markets, gourmet emporiums and local specialities in whatever country I visit. The timing of this trip coincided with a rather intriguing gastronomic tour of Spain run by Tony Tan, a fellow Australian chef and food writer with a penchant for all things Spanish. I was on that plane before you could say 'paella', bound for magical Madrid. Within hours of landing I was sampling some excellent tapas and a glass or two of *vino tinto* with new friends. It was the start of something beautiful — a love affair with Spanish food.

I'm honoured to have had the opportunity to dine at some wonderful establishments the world over but some of the meals on that trip, without a hint of exaggeration, were the best of my life. Incredible, artistic, technically perfect, fascinating dishes that tasted of concentrated raw passion. Boundaries were successfully being pushed across boundaries. There appeared to be a fierce, unspoken competition to hunt down the freshest of fresh — the pride in sourcing quality produce and in creating superior fare was intense. The flavours, textures and presentation — whether a perfect version of a rustic dish, a modern play on the traditional or a Spanish take on international specialities — could not be faulted. I was ecstatic. I had read and heard that things had hotted up in Spanish kitchens, but what I found far exceeded my expectations. Perhaps Spain was indeed the new Foodie Nirvana?

Spain's colour and passion has always overflowed into all aspects of life and translates naturally into her rustic, hearty cuisine, but today Spanish food is undergoing an evolution. Grassroots style has been shaken up with a dash of funky cool, resulting in a superb new cuisine offshoot full of fun and flavour.

The recipes in this book were inspired by the amazing meals I feasted on during this indulgent culinary fantasy. The three chapters are based on the way the Spanish like to eat. The first, Tasca, relates to tapas bars, where friends can share a few small tasting plates over a drink, or enjoy a complete meal with the addition of a few extra plates. In this chapter you will find many new tapas ideas — some a little exotic, others more familiar with a small twist.

The second chapter, Cocina, means both 'kitchen' and 'cooking'. Traditionally, most Spaniards eat their main meals at home, and this chapter features updated versions of homestyle dishes, some with subtle changes to the authentic dish, others made more elegant and refined based on the original flavour or idea.

And finally, Postres. There are few standard desserts on traditional Spanish restaurant menus but in contemporary establishments, one could be forgiven for thinking the Spanish are connoisseurs of sweet. Again, my recipes are a play on the original and incorporate the flavours of Spain into modern, delicious forms.

I am so happy to be sharing some exciting new Spanish food experiences with you. I hope that with these recipes you are able to enjoy a little taste of what I was fortunate enough to discover in my travels to Spain.

tasca

Although almonds — particularly the delicate-textured marcona variety — are enjoyed all over Spain in many incarnations, they are often eaten simply toasted and salted with a glass of chilled fino (dry) sherry. This lightly spiced version is very moreish.

smoky fried almonds

20 g (³/₄ oz) butter
60 ml (2 fl oz/¹/₄ cup) olive oil
2 garlic cloves, bruised
235 g (8¹/₂ oz/1¹/₂ cups) blanched almonds,
    preferably Spanish (such as marcona)
2¹/₂ teaspoons sea salt, lightly crushed
1 teaspoon caster (superfine) sugar
1 teaspoon smoked sweet paprika
¹/₂ teaspoon ground oregano
cayenne pepper, to taste

Makes about 250 g (9 oz/1¹/₂ cups)

Melt the butter and oil in a small frying pan over medium heat. Add the garlic and almonds and stir constantly for 4–5 minutes, or until golden.

Remove the almonds with a slotted spoon and drain briefly on crumpled paper towels. Mix the salt, sugar, paprika, oregano and cayenne pepper in a bowl, then add the almonds and toss to coat. Spread the almonds on a tray and allow to cool to room temperature. Serve in a small bowl to nibble on with drinks.

These 'cigars' are a play on those Spanish salt cod fritters, *buñuelos de bacalao*. Here you can really taste the creamy, garlicky filling as you crunch into the golden pastry. Freezing prior to cooking ensures the filling doesn't get too hot, so they don't burst.

bacalao cigars

250 g (9 oz) bacalao (dried salt cod)
125 ml (4 fl oz/$\frac{1}{2}$ cup) fino (dry) sherry or white wine
1 fresh bay leaf
1 x 200 g (7 oz) floury potato, such as russet (idaho)
    or king edward, peeled and chopped
375 ml (13 fl oz/1$\frac{1}{2}$ cups) cream (whipping)
1 teaspoon finely chopped thyme
6 garlic cloves, crushed
1 small handful flat-leaf (Italian) parsley, chopped
6 sheets filo pastry, each measuring about 24 x 48 cm
    (9$\frac{1}{2}$ x 19 inches)
1 egg, beaten
olive oil, for deep-frying
lemon wedges, to serve

Makes 12

Soak the cod in cold water in the refrigerator for 24 hours, changing the water several times. Drain the fish well.

Bring a saucepan of water to the boil. Add the cod, sherry and bay leaf and allow to come to the boil again. Reduce the heat and simmer for 35 minutes, or until the fish is tender and starting to flake. Remove the pan from the heat, allow to cool to room temperature, then drain.

Meanwhile, cook the potato in a small saucepan of boiling water for 10 minutes, or until tender, then drain and mash.

Remove the skin and any bones from the cod, then mash the flesh with a fork. Put the cod in a small saucepan and mix in the cream, thyme, garlic and potato. Simmer for 30 minutes, stirring regularly until a thick paste forms. Remove from the heat and allow to cool to room temperature, then stir in the parsley. Refrigerate for 1$\frac{1}{2}$ hours, or until completely cold.

Roll heaped tablespoons of the mixture into 12 cigar shapes about 10 cm (4 inches) long. Cut each filo sheet in half into two squares, and place inside a folded tea towel (dish towel) to stop them drying out. Lay a pastry square on the work surface so that one corner is facing you. Lay a cod cigar horizontally along the nearest pastry corner and gently roll the parcel up, tucking in the sides about halfway up. Brush the end flap of the filo with the beaten egg, then press together. Repeat with the remaining filo sheets and cod mixture to make 12 cigars. Freeze for at least 1 hour before cooking.

When you're ready to cook, fill a deep-fryer or large heavy-based saucepan one-third full of oil and heat to 180°C (350°F), or until a cube of bread dropped into the oil browns in 15 seconds. Deep-fry the cigars, three or four at a time, for about 2–3 minutes, or until crisp and golden. Drain on crumpled paper towels and serve hot, with lemon wedges.

With their wonderful combination of flavours, these simple bites are delightful baked and served warm, but in summer, when the last thing you want to do is turn on the oven, you don't even need to heat them — simply roll them up and nibble away.

dates with blue cheese and jamón

12 fresh dates
120 g (4¼ oz) firm, creamy blue cheese
    (preferably Spanish), cut into 12 even pieces
6 small guindilla chillies in vinegar (see Note),
    cut in half across the middle
12 thin slices best-quality jamón or prosciutto,
    about 120 g (4¼ oz) in total
olive oil, for brushing

Makes 12

Preheat the oven to 190°C (375°F/Gas 5). Cut a slit in the dates and carefully remove the stones. Insert a piece of cheese into each slit, then a guindilla half. Wrap a piece of jamón around each date, making sure the end flap is tucked neatly underneath and that the strip of jamón is not too wide so you can still see the dates at either end. Brush with a little oil (if you are not baking the dates, you can omit this step).

Put the dates on a baking tray, seam side down, and bake for 10 minutes, or until the dates are warmed through and the cheese has softened. Serve at once, with a slightly sweet sherry such as manzanilla.

Note: If you are unable to obtain guindilla chillies, you could instead use jalapeño chillies in vinegar. When in season, ripe fresh figs can be used instead of the dates — simply cut them in half, then fill with the cheese and chillies and wrap with the jamón before eating as is, or baking them.

Cava, a Champagne-style sparkling Spanish wine, is delicious with tapas if sherry isn't your tipple of choice. It also makes a wonderful fresh, zingy dressing for these slightly sweet, smoky grilled oysters.

oysters with cava dressing

cava dressing
60 ml (2 fl oz/1/4 cup) Cava or sparkling white wine
2 teaspoons sherry vinegar
3 teaspoons finely chopped red onion
1 tablespoon finely chopped flat-leaf (Italian) parsley

24 oysters, on the half-shell
50 g (1 3/4 oz) butter, melted
2 slices jamón, prosciutto or jambon, finely chopped
1/2 teaspoon caster (superfine) sugar

Makes 24

Put all the Cava dressing ingredients in a small bowl. Mix well, then season to taste and set aside for 15 minutes for the flavours to infuse.

Meanwhile, preheat the grill (broiler) to high. Sit the oysters on a baking tray. Mix together the melted butter, jamón and sugar and spoon the mixture over the oysters. Grill (broil) the oysters for 1 1/2 minutes, or until the jamón is a little crispy. Remove from the heat, drizzle each oyster with the dressing and serve immediately — with a glass of chilled Cava, of course!

Prawns smothered in a garlicky sauce are a tapas staple. This version is enhanced with the added flavour of rich, paprika-spiced chorizo, smoky dried chillies and a dash of sherry.

garlic prawns with chorizo

6 garlic cloves
50 g (1¾ oz) butter
2 tablespoons olive oil
1 chorizo sausage, cut into 1 cm (½ inch) cubes
3 small dried, smoked red chillies, preferably
    red guindilla chillies if available
12 raw king prawns (shrimp), peeled and deveined,
    tails intact
1 tablespoon fino (dry) sherry
crusty bread rolls, to serve

Serves 4

Finely chop four of the garlic cloves and set aside. Finely slice the rest.

Melt the butter and oil in a large saucepan over low heat. Add the sliced garlic and cook, stirring, for 4 minutes, or until golden. Remove from the pan with a slotted spoon and drain on crumpled paper towels. Increase the heat to medium–high and cook the chorizo and whole chillies, stirring, for 3 minutes, or until the chorizo becomes crispy and fragrant.

Add the chopped garlic and fry for 1 minute, or until lightly golden, then add the prawns and sherry and cook for 2 minutes, or until the prawns turn pink and curl.

Toss the crispy garlic slices through the prawns and season to taste. Turn out into a small bowl and serve with crusty bread rolls for mopping up the garlicky juices.

Crisp little croquettes are a tapas favourite. They can feature a variety of fillings, but are always bound together by a thick, creamy béchamel sauce. Here, ground almonds and breadcrumbs give the crisp, golden coating extra flavour and a nutty crunch.

croquetas de pollo

béchamel sauce
90 g (3¹/₄ oz) butter
90 g (3¹/₄ oz/³/₄ cup) plain (all-purpose) flour
1 tablespoon fino (dry) sherry
125 ml (4 fl oz/¹/₂ cup) home-made or low-salt
    chicken stock
1 fresh bay leaf
185 ml (6 fl oz/³/₄ cup) milk
60 ml (2 fl oz/¹/₄ cup) cream (whipping)

filling
2 teaspoons olive oil
¹/₂ leek, white part only, finely chopped
3 slices jamón, prosciutto or jambon, finely chopped
¹/₂ celery stalk, very finely diced
200 g (7 oz) minced (ground) chicken
2 tablespoons finely chopped flat-leaf (Italian) parsley

50 g (1³/₄ oz/¹/₂ cup) seasoned dry fine breadcrumbs
55 g (2 oz/¹/₂ cup) ground almonds
seasoned plain (all-purpose) flour, for coating
2 eggs, lightly beaten
olive oil, for deep-frying
2 teaspoons sweet or smoked sweet paprika,
    mixed with 1 tablespoon salt
lemon wedges, to serve

Makes 24

To make the béchamel sauce, melt the butter in a saucepan over medium heat, then add the flour and stir for about 5 minutes, or until the mixture is dry and a little crumbly and smells like pastry cooking. Add the sherry and stir until absorbed. Remove from the heat and gradually whisk in the stock. Add the bay leaf, gradually whisk in about half the milk, then return to the heat and whisk in the rest of the milk, then the cream. Cook, stirring, for 8–10 minutes, or until the mixture is very thick and smooth and starts to pull away from the side of the pan. Remove from the heat and set aside.

To make the filling, heat the oil in a frying pan over medium heat. Add the leek, jamón and celery and cook for 5 minutes, or until softened and lightly golden. Add the chicken, breaking up any lumps with the back of a spoon, and fry until the chicken changes colour and is just cooked through. Transfer the mixture to a bowl. Remove the bay leaf from the béchamel sauce and add the sauce to the chicken along with the parsley. Mix well, season to taste, then cover and refrigerate for 3 hours, or until completely cold.

Divide the filling into 24 portions and roll into small croquette shapes 5–6 cm (2–2¹/₂ inches) long. Combine the breadcrumbs and ground almonds in a small bowl. Lightly coat the croquettes in the flour, dip them in the beaten egg, allowing any excess to drip off, then coat them in the breadcrumb mixture. Sit the croquettes in a single layer on a tray and refrigerate for 2 hours, or until ready to cook.

Fill a deep-fryer or large heavy-based saucepan one-third full of oil and heat to 180°C (350°F), or until a cube of bread dropped into the oil browns in 15 seconds. Deep-fry the croquettes in three batches for 2–3 minutes at a time, or until lightly golden. Drain well on crumpled paper towels and serve hot with the paprika salt and lemon wedges.

Variation: Instead of the chicken, try using minced (ground) pork, flaked tuna or finely chopped and sautéed garlic mushrooms, and add different herbs to taste. Also, instead of the lemon wedges, the croquettes can be served with a small bowl of sherry vinegar for dipping into.

In this famous dish, large slices of slow-cooked octopus tentacles are drizzled with good olive oil and a sprinkling of smoky paprika. I have used naturally tender baby octopus and added fresh parsley and a lemon dressing for a refreshing zip.

galician octopus

500 g (1 lb 2 oz) baby octopus (see Note)
2 tablespoons sherry vinegar
80 ml (2½ fl oz/⅓ cup) extra virgin olive oil
1 teaspoon smoked sweet paprika
2 garlic cloves, crushed
2 teaspoons grated lemon zest
1 tablespoon lemon juice
3 teaspoons sherry vinegar, extra
½ red onion, cut into thin wedges
1 large handful flat-leaf (Italian) parsley, roughly chopped
extra smoked sweet paprika (optional), for sprinkling

Serves 4–6

Using a small, sharp knife, carefully cut between the head and tentacles of each octopus, just below the eyes. Grasp the body of the octopus and push the beak out and up through the centre of the tentacles with your finger. Cut the eyes from the head of the octopus by slicing a small disc off and discard the eye section. To clean the octopus head, carefully slit through one side, avoiding the ink sac, and scrape out any gut from inside. Rinse under running water to remove any remaining gut.

Put the baby octopus in a saucepan of cold water with the sherry vinegar. Bring to the boil, then immediately reduce the heat to a simmer. Cook for 30 minutes, or until the octopus is very tender. Drain well.

Mix together the oil, paprika, garlic, lemon zest, lemon juice and extra sherry vinegar, then toss through the warm octopus along with the onion. Leave to cool for 10 minutes, stirring occasionally. Toss through the parsley, season to taste and serve sprinkled with a little extra smoked paprika if desired. This dish can also be served chilled.

Note: If you don't have time to clean the baby octopus, buy 350 g (12 oz) of cleaned baby octopus instead.

The basic *buñuelo* is the Spanish version of choux pastry. This crispy bite is great for handing around with drinks and is easily jazzed up by adding different spices, herbs or finely chopped jamón or chorizo.

manchego and cumin buñuelos

60 ml (2 fl oz/¹/₄ cup) extra virgin olive oil
60 g (2¹/₄ oz/¹/₂ cup) plain (all-purpose) flour, sifted
1¹/₂ teaspoons ground cumin
¹/₂ teaspoon ground oregano
¹/₈ teaspoon cayenne pepper
¹/₂ teaspoon smoked sweet paprika
1¹/₂ teaspoons very finely chopped thyme
olive oil, for deep-frying
2 large eggs, at room temperature, lightly beaten
60 g (2¹/₄ oz/²/₃ cup) finely grated Manchego cheese

Makes about 24

Put the extra virgin olive oil in a small heavy-based saucepan with 90 ml (3 fl oz) of water and 1 teaspoon of salt. Bring just to the boil over high heat, then remove from the heat and immediately tip in the flour, cumin, oregano, cayenne pepper, paprika and thyme and stir for 1 minute, or until the mixture forms a smooth paste and comes away from the side of the pan.

Put the pan back over medium heat and cook, stirring vigorously and continuously, for 5 minutes — a 'film' should start to coat the bottom of the pan, but if the oil starts to separate, the mixture is overheated and you will need to start again.

Meanwhile, fill a deep-fryer or large heavy-based saucepan one-third full of oil and heat to 165–170°C (315–325°F), or until a cube of bread dropped into the oil browns in 20–25 seconds.

Take the flour mixture from the heat, allow to cool slightly, then gradually beat in the eggs with a wooden spoon until very well combined. Continue beating for a few minutes, until the mixture becomes thick, glossy and smooth. Mix in the cheese.

Working in several batches, drop slightly heaped teaspoons of the warm *buñuelo* mixture into the oil and cook for 7 minutes — they will become puffed and golden before this time, but be sure to leave them in for the full 7 minutes so they don't collapse on cooling. Drain well on crumpled paper towels and serve immediately.

Note: Choux pastry can be temperamental so it is important to measure the ingredients precisely and to follow the method carefully.

Olives are synonymous with Spain. After curing, these luscious fruits are often used in Spanish cookery, but more commonly enjoyed as is. Olives are also wonderful marinated. Try these two delicious recipes, then experiment with your own herbs and spices.

green olives with fennel

2 garlic cloves, sliced
2 tablespoons sherry vinegar
375 g (13 oz/2$\frac{1}{2}$ cups) drained large green olives in brine
2 tablespoons fennel seeds
375 ml (13 fl oz/1$\frac{1}{2}$ cups) olive oil
3 fresh bay leaves
5 small dried, smoked red chillies, sliced
1$\frac{1}{2}$ teaspoons grated lemon zest

Makes a 700 ml (24 fl oz) jar of olives
(total weight 725 g/1 lb 9$\frac{1}{2}$ oz)

Put the garlic and sherry vinegar in a small bowl and leave to steep for 2 hours, then drain. Rinse the olives well, then spread out on a clean tea towel (dish towel) to dry.

Dry-fry the fennel seeds in a small saucepan over medium heat for 1$\frac{1}{2}$ minutes, or until fragrant. Lightly crush using a mortar and pestle or spice mill.

Put the oil, steeped garlic, fennel seeds, bay leaves, chillies and lemon zest in a small saucepan over medium heat for 2–3 minutes, or until the oil just starts to bubble. Remove from the heat and allow to cool.

Pour a little of the oil mixture into a clean 700 ml (24 fl oz) jar, add the olives, then pour in the rest of the oil mixture. Screw the lid on tightly and shake gently to mix. Store in the refrigerator for 1–2 weeks before opening to allow the flavours to develop, shaking occasionally to mix. Once the jar has been opened, the olives will keep for 2 weeks in the refrigerator.

roasted black olives

225 g (8 oz/1$\frac{1}{4}$ cups) meaty black Spanish olives
2 tablespoons olive oil
3 teaspoons finely chopped thyme
5 garlic cloves, sliced

Makes a 250 ml (9 fl oz/1 cup) jar of olives
(total weight 125 g/4$\frac{1}{2}$ oz)

Preheat the oven to 200°C (400°F/Gas 6). Rinse and drain the olives well, then place in a bowl with the oil, thyme and garlic. Mix well.

Spread the olives on a baking tray and roast for 20–25 minutes, or until the olives have shrivelled and the garlic is golden but not burnt, shaking the tray occasionally. Serve warm or at room temperature.

Note: To store any leftover olives, cover them with olive oil and refrigerate in an airtight container. They will keep for about 2 weeks.

Some of my favourite tapas are those with a crunchy coating and soft creamy filling, and this is definitely one of them — delicately flavoured with fresh fennel wrapped inside a sweet roasted baby pimiento, lightly cloaked in a crisp beer batter. Heaven.

pimientos rellenos

24 *pimientos del piquillo*
90 g (3¼ oz) butter
½ red onion, very finely chopped
¼ fennel bulb (about 60 g/2¼ oz), very finely chopped, plus 3 teaspoons finely chopped fennel fronds
3 garlic cloves, very finely chopped
90 g (3¼ oz/¾ cup) plain (all-purpose) flour
1½ tablespoons fino (dry) sherry
250 ml (9 fl oz/1 cup) milk
350 g (12 oz) best-quality tinned white tuna (*atun blanco* or *bonito del norte*) in olive oil, drained well and mashed with a fork
freshly ground white pepper, to taste
60 g (2¼ oz/⅔ cup) grated Manchego cheese
olive oil, for deep-frying
plain (all-purpose) flour, extra, for coating
lemon wedges, to serve

beer batter
125 g (4½ oz/1 cup) plain (all-purpose) flour
1 teaspoon salt
large pinch of cayenne pepper
310 ml (10¾ fl oz/1¼ cups) Spanish beer, or other pale, light-flavoured beer, at room temperature

Makes 24

Drain the pimientos well and set aside to dry.

Heat the butter in a saucepan over medium–low heat. Add the onion and chopped fennel bulb and cook for 15 minutes, or until very soft, stirring occasionally. Stir in the garlic. Increase the heat to medium, add the flour and cook for 2 minutes, stirring. Gradually stir in the sherry. Take off the heat, gradually whisk in half the milk, then return to the heat and whisk in the remaining milk. Stir for about 5 minutes, or until the sauce is smooth and very thick and leaves the side of the pan. Add the tuna and season to taste with salt and white pepper. Remove from the heat, leave to cool to room temperature, then cover and refrigerate for 1½ hours, or until completely cold. Stir through the fennel fronds and cheese and mix well.

Fill the pimiento cavities with the tuna mixture, gently pressing the filling into the tips, being careful not to split them. Refrigerate until ready to cook.

Fill a deep-fryer or large heavy-based saucepan one-third full of oil and heat to 180°C (350°F), or until a cube of bread dropped into the oil browns in 15 seconds.

Meanwhile, make the beer batter. Put the flour, salt and cayenne pepper in a bowl, then gradually whisk in the beer to make a smooth batter.

Lightly coat the pimientos in flour, then dip them in the batter, allowing any excess to drip off. Deep-fry them, four or five at a time, for about 3 minutes, or until crisp and golden and heated through. The coating should look a little see-through in parts. Serve at once with lemon wedges.

Unless you are in a flash city bar or nightclub in Spain you are unlikely to stumble across a huge variety of cocktails. However, the Spanish produce such excellent liqueurs, spirits and even cider that it would be a shame not to dress them up for a party!

cava cocktail

125 ml (4 fl oz/1/2 cup) Licor 43
6 long strips of orange zest
natural vanilla extract, to taste
750 ml (26 fl oz) bottle Cava, well chilled

Serves 6

Pour 1 tablespoon of the liqueur into six chilled champagne glasses. Give each strip of orange zest a twist to release the natural oil and place one in each glass. Add a few drops of vanilla extract to each glass and slowly top up with Cava. Serve at once.

spiced sidra

1.5 litres (52 fl oz/6 cups) bottled sweet or dry Spanish
    sidra, or other alcoholic apple cider
3 long strips of orange zest
1 cinnamon stick
2 cloves
3 teaspoons fennel seeds
1 1/2 tablespoons honey, or to taste

Serves 8

Pour 375 ml (13 fl oz/1 1/2 cups) of the cider into a small saucepan. Add the orange zest, cinnamon stick, cloves, fennel seeds and honey and stir over medium heat until the honey has melted. Bring to the boil and allow to boil for 5 minutes, then remove from the heat and cool to room temperature. (To serve cold, pour into a large pitcher, stir in the remaining cider and refrigerate for 3 hours, or until completely cold. Strain if you wish, then pour into a large serving pitcher and serve with eight small glasses.) To serve warm, pour the remaining cider into the saucepan of spiced cider and leave at room temperature for 1 hour for the flavours to infuse. Gently warm over low heat (don't let the cider boil or you will cook out the alcohol), then strain if you wish and serve.

fennel gazpacho chiller

4 very ripe tomatoes (about 400 g/14 oz in total)
1/2 small red capsicum (pepper)
1 small Lebanese (short) cucumber
1 small fennel bulb (about 150 g/5 1/2 oz), plus
    1 tablespoon chopped fennel fronds, and
    8 small strips of fennel, to garnish
2 small garlic cloves
1 small handful flat-leaf (Italian) parsley
2 teaspoons lemon juice
125 ml (4 fl oz/1/2 cup) chilli vodka or plain vodka,
    well chilled

Serves 8

Chop the tomatoes, capsicum, cucumber and fennel bulb and place in a food processor with the fennel fronds, garlic, parsley, lemon juice and a large pinch of salt. Blend until smooth. Pour the mixture through a sieve into a pitcher, pressing down on the solids to release as much liquid as possible. Discard the solids. Refrigerate for 2–3 hours, or until well chilled.

Just before serving, stir in the vodka, pour into eight small glasses and garnish each with a strip of fennel. Serve at once.

These small, decadent sandwiches are addictive. If you can't get hold of foie gras, a good-quality duck or chicken liver pâté will do. Foie gras is quite widely used in Spain, particularly in the north on account of its proximity to France.

foie gras bocadillo with sticky muscatels

sticky muscatels
10 g (1/4 oz) butter
1/2 small red onion, finely chopped
200 g (7 oz) bunch dried muscatels, plucked
    (or 1 1/4 cups plucked muscatels)
170 ml (5 1/2 fl oz/2/3 cup) Pedro Ximénez sherry
1 1/2 tablespoons sherry vinegar
125 ml (4 fl oz/1/2 cup) home-made or low-salt
    chicken stock
1 tablespoon soft brown sugar

12 small, soft, slightly crusty dinner rolls
250 g (9 oz) good-quality foie gras
1 handful micro salad greens, tiny baby rocket (arugula)
    leaves or baby green salad leaves

Makes 12

To make the sticky muscatels, first melt the butter in a small saucepan over medium–high heat. Add the onion and cook for 8 minutes, or until golden, stirring occasionally. Add the muscatels, sherry, sherry vinegar, stock and sugar. Bring to the boil, then reduce the heat and simmer for 45 minutes, or until the muscatels are plump, and the liquid is very syrupy and almost evaporated. Cool to room temperature. Makes 320 g (11 1/4 oz/1 1/3 cups).

Cut through the rolls, leaving them hinged at one side. Spread a little foie gras onto both cut sides of each roll, then fill each with six to eight muscatels and a little bundle of tiny salad greens. Serve at once.

Note: You may not need all the muscatels for these rolls, but any leftover muscatels make a stylish addition to any cheese platter — or you could use them as an accompaniment to the Spanish-style duck rillette on page 75.

Simply grilled seafood with a squeeze of fresh lemon is always lovely, but with sweet, smoky romesco sauce it is nothing less than superb. Romesco sauce is also wonderful with meats and poultry and makes a delicious dip for bread and vegetables.

barbecued seafood skewers with romesco sauce

romesco sauce

80 ml (2$^{1}/_{2}$ fl oz/$^{1}/_{3}$ cup) fruity or low-acid
    extra virgin olive oil
10 hazelnuts
10 blanched almonds
1 slice white bread, crusts removed
5 *pimientos del piquillo* (about 100 g/3$^{1}/_{2}$ oz in total)
$^{1}/_{4}$ teaspoon smoked sweet paprika
small pinch of cayenne pepper
4 garlic cloves
2 teaspoons sherry vinegar
1 ripe tomato, peeled, seeded and chopped

12 scallops, without roe
6 asparagus spears, each cut into 4 lengths to
    give 24 pieces, lightly blanched
12 raw prawns (shrimp), peeled and deveined,
    tails intact
8 spring onions (scallions), white part only,
    each cut into 4 lengths to give 24 pieces
olive oil, for brushing
small lemon wedges, to serve

Makes 12

Soak 12 wooden skewers or trimmed bay leaf twigs (see Note) in cold water for 2 hours to prevent scorching.

Meanwhile, make the romesco sauce. Put 2 tablespoons of the oil in a small saucepan over medium–low heat. Add the hazelnuts and almonds and cook, stirring, for 5 minutes, or until golden. Remove the nuts and drain on crumpled paper towels. Add the bread to the pan and fry for 2 minutes on each side, or until golden. Allow to cool slightly, then place in a food processor with the nuts, pimientos, paprika, cayenne pepper, garlic, sherry vinegar, tomato and remaining oil. Blend to a paste, and season to taste. Makes about 240 g (8$^{1}/_{2}$ oz/1 cup).

Slice or pull off any vein, membrane or hard white muscle from the scallops. Rinse the scallops and pat dry with paper towels. Thread two pieces of spring onion onto a skewer. Curl up a prawn so the ends meet, and thread it onto the skewer. Thread on two pieces of asparagus, then a scallop. Repeat with the remaining ingredients to make 12 skewers.

Heat a barbecue grill plate or chargrill pan to medium–high. Lightly brush the seafood skewers with a little oil and sprinkle with salt. Cook for 1–2 minutes on each side, or until the seafood is just cooked through. Serve at once with lemon wedges and a bowl of romesco sauce.

Note: To add a rustic touch, we've used bay leaf twigs as skewers in this recipe. They don't affect the flavour of the seafood. If you wish to use them, simply trim the leaves off 12 sturdy bay leaf twigs, trim one end of each twig to a sharp point for skewering the seafood, and follow the recipe as normal.

Sipping this intensely flavoured mushroom soup from small cups or glasses allows you to appreciate its incredible aromas. To make a real splash at your next cocktail party, present the soup in shot glasses, in which case it will serve at least 12 people.

rich mushroom soup with truffle oil

6 dried cep mushroom pieces
800 ml (28 fl oz) home-made or low-salt chicken stock
20 g ($^3/_4$ oz) butter
3 garlic cloves, very finely chopped
1 leek, white part only, finely chopped
2 slices jamón, prosciutto or jambon, finely chopped
2 tablespoons manzanilla sherry
400 g (14 oz) mixed seasonal mushrooms,
    such as Swiss brown, portobello, shiitake,
    pine or field mushrooms, chopped
150 ml (5 fl oz) cream (whipping)
black truffle oil, for drizzling

Serves 6

Put the ceps in a saucepan with 625 ml ($21^1/_2$ fl oz/$2^1/_2$ cups) of the stock and bring to the boil. Reduce the heat and simmer for 5 minutes, then turn off the heat and allow to cool. Reserving the stock, remove the ceps and chop them.

Melt the butter in a saucepan over medium–low heat. Add the garlic and leek and cook for 5 minutes, stirring now and then, until very soft and just starting to caramelize. Add the ceps, jamón, sherry, fresh mushrooms and a pinch of salt and fry, stirring occasionally, for about 6 minutes, or until the mushrooms soften.

Add the reserved mushroom stock, bring to the boil, and allow to boil for 10 minutes. Remove from the heat, allow the mixture to cool a little, then transfer to a food processor and blend until smooth. Stir in the cream and gently reheat, adding the remaining stock if the soup is too thick. Season to taste, then pour into six 125 ml (4 fl oz/$^1/_2$ cup) glasses or cups. Drizzle with a little truffle oil and serve.

Like pizza, this flat, open tart can have a thick, leavened crust, but I like a thin, crispy base, flavoured here with cumin, thyme and lemon. Coca isn't topped with cheese, but if you can't go without, sprinkle with grated Manchego or crumbled goat's cheese.

coca

caramelized onion
125 ml (4 fl oz/^{1}/$_{2}$ cup) olive oil
4 large red onions, finely sliced
125 ml (4 fl oz/^{1}/$_{2}$ cup) manzanilla sherry
2 tablespoons sherry vinegar
3 teaspoons sugar

pastry base
250 g (9 oz/2 cups) plain (all-purpose) flour
1 teaspoon finely grated lemon zest
3 teaspoons cumin seeds
3 teaspoons chopped thyme
1 teaspoon salt
80 ml (2^{1}/$_{2}$ fl oz/^{1}/$_{3}$ cup) olive oil

topping
2 tablespoons tomato paste (concentrated purée)
3 garlic cloves, crushed
1^{1}/$_{2}$ teaspoons sweet paprika
^{1}/$_{4}$ teaspoon cayenne pepper
5 *pimientos del piquillo* (about 60 g/2^{1}/$_{4}$ oz),
   cut into thin strips
6 slices jamón, prosciutto or jambon, roughly sliced
2 tablespoons baby capers, rinsed and squeezed dry
4 anchovies, cut into very thin slivers
1 tablespoon finely chopped flat-leaf (Italian) parsley

Makes 16 pieces

To caramelize the onion, heat the oil in a saucepan over medium–low heat, then add the onion and a good pinch of salt and cook, stirring occasionally, for about 40 minutes, or until the onion is lightly golden. Add the sherry, sherry vinegar and sugar and reduce the heat to low. Cook, stirring regularly, for another 1^{1}/$_{4}$ hours, or until the onion is deep golden and well caramelized — be patient, it needs to cook slowly for the best results. Leave to cool, then pour off and reserve the excess oil.

While the onion is caramelizing, make the pastry base. Sift the flour into a bowl and stir in the lemon zest, cumin seeds, thyme and salt. Make a well in the centre, then add the oil and 100 ml (3^{1}/$_{2}$ fl oz) of water. Mix thoroughly to combine, adding an extra tablespoon of water if needed. Bring the dough together into a ball, knead on a lightly floured surface for a few minutes, then cover with plastic wrap and refrigerate for at least 1 hour.

Preheat the oven to 220°C (425°F/Gas 7). Roll the dough out until it is large enough to cover a 32 cm (12^{3}/$_{4}$ inch) square (or large rectangular) baking tray — the dough will only be about 2–3 mm (^{1}/$_{16}$–^{1}/$_{8}$ inch) thick. Put the pastry on the baking tray and trim the edges, patching any gaps with pastry scraps if necessary. Bake for 8 minutes, or until lightly golden, then remove and allow to cool slightly. Turn the oven temperature down to 190°C (375°F/Gas 5).

To assemble the topping, combine the tomato paste, garlic, paprika and cayenne pepper. In a small bowl, toss the pimientos, jamón, capers and anchovies with 1 tablespoon of the reserved onion oil to coat. Spread the tomato paste mixture over the pastry base, leaving a 5 mm (^{1}/$_{4}$ inch) border, then spread the caramelized onion evenly over the top. Scatter with the jamón mixture and bake for 20–25 minutes, or until the base is crispy and golden and has shrunk away from the edge of the tray. Sprinkle the parsley over the top, cut into portions and serve.

Squid needs to be cooked in hot oil for only a brief time or it will lose its tenderness. The accompanying garlicky saffron allioli is given a fresh twist with the addition of crisp, slightly tart yet distinctly sweet green apple.

crisp squid with saffron and green apple allioli

saffron and green apple allioli
small pinch of saffron threads
1 tablespoon lemon juice
80 ml (2½ fl oz/⅓ cup) allioli (see Basics, page 187)
½ crisp green apple, cored but not peeled,
    very finely diced

300 g (10½ oz) cleaned squid (see Note)
olive oil, for deep-frying
well-seasoned plain (all-purpose) flour, for coating

Serves 4–6

To make the saffron and green apple allioli, put the saffron and lemon juice in a small saucepan and allow to just come to the boil. Quickly remove from the heat and set aside for 10 minutes, swirling occasionally, or until the saffron has coloured the liquid a dark golden colour and the mixture has cooled. Stir in the allioli and apple, mixing well to distribute the saffron colour, then transfer to a serving bowl and set aside.

Rinse the squid under cold running water and pat dry with paper towels. Cut the tubes along one side and open them out into a flat piece. With a sharp knife, lightly score the inside surface with crisscross lines to make the squid curl up during cooking — don't cut too deeply, just enough to mark the flesh. Slice into 4 cm (1½ inch) squares.

Fill a deep-fryer or large heavy-based saucepan one-third full of oil and heat to 180°C (350°F), or until a cube of bread dropped into the oil browns in 15 seconds.

Working in two batches, toss the squid with the flour until lightly coated, shaking off any excess, then deep-fry for 1–2 minutes, or until lightly golden. Drain well on crumpled paper towels, season well and serve at once with the allioli.

Note: In this recipe we also used a few cleaned tentacles, which fishmongers may give you when you ask for cleaned squid. To prepare the tentacles, simply cut away the tops to remove any innards that may still be attached, then slice them into two pieces down the middle, removing the beak. Then continue as for the squid tubes (you won't need to score them).

Empanadas are a type of Spanish pie with many different fillings. Here, pork and sweet onions are simmered in a tomatoey sauce with cinnamon, cumin and pine nuts, then wrapped into small delectable pastries. Any leftovers make a special picnic treat.

sweet pork empanadas

filling
2 x 300 g (10½ oz) pork loin chops (ask your
    butcher for the centre-cut chops)
½ red onion, finely chopped
2 garlic cloves, crushed
½ teaspoon ground cinnamon
½ teaspoon sweet paprika
½ teaspoon ground cumin
pinch of cayenne pepper
125 ml (4 fl oz/½ cup) white wine
250 ml (9 fl oz/1 cup) home-made or low-salt
    chicken stock
1 tablespoon cider vinegar
1½ tablespoons tomato paste (concentrated purée)
1 tablespoon soft brown sugar
3 *pimientos del piquillo*, finely sliced
1½ tablespoons pine nuts, toasted
1 tablespoon finely chopped coriander (cilantro) leaves

pastry
400 g (14 oz/3¼ cups) plain (all-purpose) flour
1 teaspoon salt
80 g (2¾ oz) butter, chilled
3 eggs
60 ml (2 fl oz/¼ cup) fino (dry) sherry

Makes 16

To make the filling, remove the skin and fat from the pork, then dice the skin and fat and put it in a saucepan over medium heat. Cook for 30 minutes, or until the solids are golden and the liquid fat is released. Discard the solids and leave about 1½ tablespoons of the fat in the pan.

Meanwhile, remove the meat from the bones — it should yield about 400 g (14 oz) — then cut the meat into 1 cm (½ inch) cubes and set aside.

Sauté the onion in the pan for 5 minutes, or until golden. Remove from the pan and set aside. Increase the heat to medium–high, then add the pork and brown in two batches for about 5 minutes at a time. Remove and set aside.

Add the garlic, cinnamon, paprika, cumin and cayenne pepper to the pan and cook for 30 seconds. Add the wine and cook for 1 minute, then stir in the stock, vinegar, tomato paste and sugar. Return the pork and onion to the pan, bring to the boil, then reduce the heat and simmer for 1 hour 10 minutes, or until the pork is very tender. Allow to cool slightly, then stir through the pimientos, pine nuts and coriander. Season to taste, then refrigerate for 2–3 hours, or until completely cold.

Meanwhile, make the pastry. Sift the flour and salt into a bowl. Grate the butter over the flour, then rub it in with your fingertips until the mixture resembles fine crumbs. Mix two of the eggs with the sherry, then 'cut' them into the mixture with a flat-bladed knife until small clumps form. Gather the dough into a ball, cover with plastic wrap and refrigerate for 30 minutes.

Lightly beat the remaining egg. Divide the dough in half, then, on a floured surface, roll out each half to a rectangle approximately 22 x 44 cm (8½ x 17½ inches) in size. Using a sharp knife and a ruler, cut out 16 pastry bases, each 11 cm (4¼ inches) square. Place a heaped tablespoon of the filling in the centre of each square and brush around the edges with a little beaten egg. Fold over the pastry to form 16 triangles, and firmly seal the edges together with a fork. Refrigerate until ready to cook.

Preheat the oven to 180°C (350°F/Gas 4). Sit the *empanadas* on baking trays lined with baking paper and brush with the remaining beaten egg. Bake for 22–25 minutes, or until the pastry is lightly golden and the filling is hot.

Fennel is such a freshly flavoured ingredient, and in this wonderful tapas dish it is used as both a herb and vegetable. The bulb is caramelized as a base for the tender scallops, and the fronds used in the aromatic dressing.

scallops with fennel and anchovy oil

12 large scallops (without roe), on the half-shell
10 g (1/4 oz) butter
2 tablespoons olive oil
2 baby fennel bulbs (200 g/7 oz in total), finely diced,
    plus 2 teaspoons chopped fennel fronds
1/2 teaspoon ground fennel seeds
80 ml (2 1/2 fl oz/1/3 cup) manzanilla sherry
60 ml (2 fl oz/1/4 cup) extra virgin olive oil
3 anchovies, finely chopped
1 garlic clove, very finely chopped
1/2 teaspoon finely grated lemon zest

Makes 12

Carefully remove the scallops from their shells — you may need to use a small, sharp knife to slice the scallops free, being careful not to leave any scallop meat behind. Reserve the shells. Slice or pull off any vein, membrane or hard white muscle, then rinse the scallops and pat dry with paper towels. Wash the shells with hot water and dry well.

Put the butter and 1 tablespoon of the olive oil in a saucepan over low heat. When the butter has melted, add the diced fennel bulb, ground fennel seeds, sherry and a pinch of salt and cook gently for 40 minutes, or until the fennel is soft and starting to caramelize. Set aside.

Put the extra virgin olive oil, anchovies, garlic, lemon zest and a pinch of salt in a small saucepan over medium heat and mash the anchovies to a paste. Cook, stirring now and then, for 5 minutes, or until the garlic is lightly golden.

Heat the remaining olive oil in a large frying pan over high heat. When the pan is very hot, add the scallops and cook for 1 minute on each side, then quickly take them off the heat.

Spoon a small amount of the caramelized fennel mixture into each scallop shell, then top with a scallop. Stir most of the fennel fronds into the anchovy mixture, reserving some as a garnish, then drizzle over the scallops. Sprinkle with the remaining fennel fronds and serve at once.

Traditional *pan con tomate* — a simple snack of toasted bread rubbed with tomato and garlic — is eaten all over Spain. I have added goat's cheese and smoky paprika, making it a little more decadent and also suitable as a light meal served with a salad.

pan con tomate with goat's cheese and paprika

3 very ripe tomatoes
1 small, crusty breadstick, about 35 cm (14 inches) long
extra virgin olive oil, for brushing
3 garlic cloves, halved
150 g (5½ oz) jar soft marinated goat's cheese feta
    in olive oil (reserve 1½ tablespoons of the oil)
2 tablespoons roughly chopped flat-leaf (Italian) parsley
smoked sweet paprika, for sprinkling

Makes 6

Preheat the grill (broiler) to high. Slice two of the tomatoes in half across the middle, then cut the other tomato into 1 cm (½ inch) cubes. Cut the bread on an angle into six slices about 1.5 cm (⅝ inch) thick, then lightly brush each slice with the extra virgin olive oil.

Grill (broil) the bread for 1 minute on each side, or until golden. Remove from the heat and immediately rub half a garlic clove over the top of each slice, then rub each slice with the cut tomato halves.

Put the toasts on a baking tray and crumble the goat's cheese over the top. Drizzle with a little of the reserved marinating oil, then grill for another 3 minutes, or until the cheese is warm and has melted a little.

Combine the diced tomato, parsley and 2 teaspoons of the reserved marinating oil and arrange the mixture over the toasts. Sprinkle with smoked paprika and drizzle with a little more reserved oil if desired. Serve immediately.

In this elegant dish, fresh sardine fillets hide an exotically flavoured filling bearing distinctly Arabic ingredients. These sardine 'sandwiches' are baked briefly and simply finished with a squeeze of lemon juice.

sardines with muscatels, mint and pine nuts

stuffing

2 tablespoons dried muscatels, or other raisins
1 tablespoon manzanilla sherry
2 tablespoons pine nuts, toasted and chopped
1$\frac{1}{2}$ teaspoons finely grated lemon zest
2 tablespoons finely chopped mint
1$\frac{1}{2}$ tablespoons finely chopped flat-leaf (Italian) parsley
2 slices jamón, prosciutto or jambon, very finely chopped
2 tablespoons very finely chopped red onion

16 sardines, cleaned and butterflied (ask your
    fishmonger to do this)
extra virgin olive oil, for drizzling
sea salt flakes, for sprinkling
lemon wedges, to serve
allioli (optional), to serve (see Basics, page 187)

Makes 16

To make the stuffing, finely chop the muscatels and put them in a small bowl with the sherry. Leave to steep for 10 minutes. Add the pine nuts, lemon zest, mint, parsley, jamón and onion, mix well and season to taste.

Preheat the oven to 200°C (400°F/Gas 6). Place eight sardines, skin side down, in a lightly oiled baking dish, opening them out into a butterfly shape. Spread about 1 tablespoon of the stuffing over each sardine, making sure they are well covered. Top with the remaining eight sardines, skin side up, to make sardine 'sandwiches'. Drizzle liberally with extra virgin olive oil and sprinkle with sea salt flakes.

Bake the sardines for 10 minutes, or until they are just cooked through. Cut each sardine 'sandwich' in half lengthways down the natural line of the fish to make 16 pieces. Serve at once with lemon wedges, and perhaps a small bowl of allioli if desired.

Tortillitas — 'little tortillas' — of prawns bound with chickpea flour seasoned with cumin, paprika and fennel are a fine example of the Moorish influence on Spanish cuisine. The beer in the dough acts as a leavening agent, making these fritters light and crispy.

prawn tortillitas with herbed yoghurt

herbed yoghurt
170 g (6 oz/²/₃ cup) sheep's milk yoghurt
2 tablespoons finely shredded mint
1¹/₂ tablespoons chopped coriander (cilantro)
1 garlic clove, crushed
2 teaspoons lemon juice

60 g (2¹/₄ oz/¹/₂ cup) plain (all-purpose) flour
55 g (2 oz/¹/₂ cup) besan (chickpea flour)
2 teaspoons ground cumin
¹/₂ teaspoon smoked sweet paprika
pinch of cayenne pepper
¹/₂ teaspoon ground fennel seeds
1 teaspoon salt
¹/₂ small red onion, very finely chopped
2 eggs
185 ml (6 fl oz/³/₄ cup) pale, light-flavoured beer,
    preferably Spanish
750 g (1 lb 10 oz) raw prawns (shrimp), peeled,
    deveined and finely chopped
oil, for pan-frying
lemon wedges, to serve

Makes about 30

To make the herbed yoghurt, put the yoghurt, mint, coriander, garlic and lemon juice in a small dipping bowl, mix well and season to taste. Set aside for the flavours to develop while making the fritters.

Combine the flour, besan, cumin, paprika, cayenne pepper, fennel and salt in a bowl and make a well in the centre. Put the onion, eggs and beer in a separate bowl and lightly beat together. Pour the mixture into the flour well, then mix to make a smooth batter. Leave to rest for 15 minutes, then stir in the chopped prawns.

Pour enough oil into a large, deep, heavy-based frying pan to cover the base by 3 mm (¹/₈ inch) and place over medium–high heat. When the oil is hot, add heaped tablespoons of the batter to the pan, flattening them slightly. Cook the *tortillitas* in batches for 2 minutes on each side, or until golden and cooked through — you should be able to cook them five at a time. Drain on crumpled paper towels, sprinkle with a little salt if desired and serve hot with the yoghurt dipping sauce.

Note: These *tortillitas* are also terrific with the saffron and green apple allioli on page 40 — just omit the apple.

Meat and seafood are often paired in Spanish cooking. White butifarra (*butifarra blanca*), a delicious fresh pork sausage often seasoned with fennel and pepper, marries well with clams, white wine and garlic.

baby clams with white butifarra

500 g (1 lb 2 oz) baby clams (vongole)
2 white butifarra sausages, or other good-quality
    fresh white pork sausages (Italian-style if you
    can't get Spanish)
1 tablespoon olive oil
10 g (¼ oz) butter
1 small leek, white part only, finely sliced
4 garlic cloves, chopped
80 ml (2½ fl oz/⅓ cup) white wine
80 ml (2½ fl oz/⅓ cup) home-made or low-salt
    chicken stock
1 small handful flat-leaf (Italian) parsley, chopped

Serves 4–6

First, soak the clams in several changes of cold water for 2 hours to remove any grit.

Skin the sausages, then break the filling up into small clumps. Heat half the oil in a large frying pan over medium heat. Add the sausage pieces and sauté for 4–5 minutes, or until lightly golden and cooked through. Remove from the pan and set aside.

Add the remaining oil to the pan with the butter, leek and garlic and cook for 2 minutes, or until the leek has softened and is lightly golden. Increase the heat to high, add the wine and stock and cook for 30 seconds, or until the liquid has almost evaporated. Add the clams and sausage and cook, shaking the pan occasionally, for 6–8 minutes, or until the clams open. Discard any clams that haven't opened by that time. Season to taste, mix the parsley through and serve immediately.

This summery sangria is superb for an *al fresco* lunch. The sweet *leche merengada* punch is a Spanish version of eggnog. Don't save it for winters around the fire — it is delightful any time and can be enjoyed by the whole family if you omit the alcohol.

watermelon and rosé sangria

125 g (4½ oz/heaped ¾ cup) ripe strawberries
300 g (10½ oz/1 cup) seeded watermelon flesh, cut into 1 cm (½ inch) cubes
1 small lime, finely sliced
1 tablespoon caster (superfine) sugar
60 ml (2 fl oz/¼ cup) Licor 43, or other orange-flavoured liqueur
750 ml (26 fl oz) bottle rosé wine, chilled
750 ml (26 fl oz/3 cups) chilled lemonade
unsprayed small fresh rose petals (optional), to garnish

Serves 8

Hull the strawberries, cut them into eighths and place in a large pitcher with the watermelon and lime slices. Sprinkle the sugar over the top, then gently pour in the liqueur. Leave at room temperature for 1 hour for the flavours to develop. Pour in the chilled wine and lemonade and stir well. Float the rose petals on top to garnish if desired, and serve.

leche merengada punch

625 ml (21½ fl oz/2½ cups) milk
145 g (5¼ oz/⅔ cup) caster (superfine) sugar
2 strips lemon zest
1 cinnamon stick
½ teaspoon natural vanilla extract
4 egg whites
ground cinnamon, for sprinkling
white rum (optional), to taste

Serves 6–8

Put the milk in a saucepan with the sugar, lemon zest, cinnamon stick and vanilla extract and place over medium heat. Bring to the boil, then reduce the heat and simmer for 20 minutes to allow the flavours to infuse.

Meanwhile, beat the egg whites to firm peaks using electric beaters. With the motor still running, gradually strain the hot milk mixture into the egg whites and beat until well combined and frothy. Pour into a chilled pitcher, leave to cool a little, then refrigerate for 1 hour, or until cold. Stir again before serving. Sprinkle with cinnamon and serve as a non-alcoholic milk punch (kids love it), or add a little white rum to taste.

A quick, delicate alternative to serving up slabs of cheese on a cheeseboard — and an excellent way to use up leftover cheese. I love the savoury–sweet flavour combination of these tartlets, particularly when the cheese is served warm, gooey and melted.

quince and three-cheese tartlets

50 g (1³/₄ oz) soft goat's cheese
40 g (1¹/₂ oz/heaped ¹/₃ cup) grated Manchego cheese
50 g (1³/₄ oz) firm, creamy, full-flavoured blue cheese, crumbled
1¹/₂ tablespoons cream (whipping)
2 eggs, lightly beaten
2 teaspoons finely chopped flat-leaf (Italian) parsley
1 teaspoon finely chopped sage
¹/₄ small red onion, grated
3 teaspoons quince paste
24 good-quality ready-made tartlet cases, about 4–5 cm (1¹/₂–2 inches) in diameter

Makes 24

Mash the goat's cheese in a bowl. Add the Manchego, blue cheese, cream, eggs, parsley and sage. Wrap the grated onion in the corner of a clean tea towel (dish towel) and squeeze with your hands to extract any excess moisture. Add the onion to the cheese mixture, stir well to combine, then season to taste.

Preheat the oven to 170°C (325°F/Gas 3). Put ¹/₈ teaspoon of quince paste in each pastry case, then divide the cheese mixture among them. Place the tartlets on a baking tray and bake for 10 minutes, or until the pastry is slightly puffed and lightly golden. Serve immediately.

Those familiar with the tapas staple *albóndigas* will know it as pork and beef meatballs in tomato sauce. This lighter version is based on the flavours of *gallina en pepitoria* — a chicken stew from La Mancha, flavoured with saffron and thickened with almonds.

chicken albóndigas with saffron almond sauce

chicken meatballs
250 g (9 oz) minced (ground) chicken
60 g (2¼ oz/¾ cup) fresh breadcrumbs
1 garlic clove, crushed
1 small egg
1½ tablespoons chopped flat-leaf (Italian) parsley
½ teaspoon finely grated lemon zest

saffron almond sauce
olive oil, for pan-frying
20 blanched almonds
½ small red onion, finely chopped
1 fresh bay leaf
2 garlic cloves, crushed
½ teaspoon ground cumin
¼ teaspoon ground cinnamon
¼ teaspoon smoked paprika
1 clove
2 tablespoons white wine
2 tablespoons manzanilla sherry
125 ml (4 fl oz/½ cup) home-made or low-salt
    chicken stock
pinch of saffron threads
1 hard-boiled egg, the yolk separated and the
    white finely diced
1 tablespoon lemon juice

Makes 12

Put all the chicken meatball ingredients in a bowl, season with salt and a little freshly ground white pepper and thoroughly mix together using your hands. Cover and refrigerate for the flavours to develop while you make the sauce.

To make the saffron almond sauce, heat 2 tablespoons of olive oil in a saucepan over medium heat, then add the almonds and cook, stirring, for 5 minutes, or until golden. Remove with a slotted spoon and drain on crumpled paper towels. Add the onion to the pan and cook for 5 minutes, or until softened and lightly golden. Add the bay leaf, garlic, cumin, cinnamon, paprika and clove and cook for 1 minute, or until fragrant. Add the wine, sherry, stock and saffron, bring to the boil and allow to boil for 5 minutes, or until reduced to about 170 ml (5½ fl oz/⅔ cup). Take the pan off the heat, discard the clove and bay leaf and set aside while cooking the meatballs.

Finely grind the almonds and egg yolk using a mortar and pestle or small food processor. Stir in the lemon juice to form a paste. Set aside.

Divide the chicken mixture into 12 portions and roll into evenly sized meatballs or patties. Heat a little oil in a large, heavy-based frying pan over medium–high heat and cook the meatballs for 12 minutes, turning occasionally, or until just cooked through and browned all over. Set aside, cover and keep warm.

Bring the saffron almond sauce to the boil again, reduce the heat to a simmer, then add the almond and egg yolk paste and stir until the sauce thickens. Season to taste. Put the meatballs in a serving dish and pour the sauce over the top, or serve it as a dipping sauce on the side. Garnish with the egg white and serve.

Note: These meatballs also make fabulous party snacks — simply roll them into 24 smaller cocktail-sized balls or patties and cook them for a shorter time.

Escalivada, a traditional Catalan side dish of smoky grilled vegetables, is the inspiration for this silky, savoury custard. Serve it warm, spooning it straight from the glass, or chill and turn out cold to enjoy as a wonderful summer vegetable pâté.

escalivada custards with manchego wafers

1 small eggplant (aubergine)
1 red capsicum (pepper), cut into quarters
1 red onion, unpeeled, cut into quarters
olive oil, for drizzling
4 garlic cloves, unpeeled
8 egg yolks
250 ml (9 fl oz/1 cup) cream (whipping)
1 teaspoon finely chopped thyme

manchego wafers
100 g (3¹/₂ oz/1¹/₄ cups) grated Manchego cheese
¹/₂ teaspoon smoked sweet paprika
1 teaspoon finely chopped thyme

Makes 6

Preheat the oven to 220°C (425°F/Gas 7). If you have a gas stovetop, skewer the eggplant with a barbecue fork and hold it directly over the open flame for about 5 minutes, or until the skin is blackened and charred all over, turning the eggplant occasionally — this will give it a wonderful smoky flavour. Alternatively, heat a barbecue chargrill plate to high and sit the eggplant on the open grill bars over the flame for about 5 minutes, or until the skin is blackened, turning occasionally.

Sit the eggplant in a baking dish with the capsicum and onion. Drizzle with oil, sprinkle with salt and bake for 40 minutes, or until the eggplant is very soft and almost collapsed. Add the garlic, cover with foil and cook for a further 10 minutes, or until the garlic is soft. Remove from the heat.

Meanwhile, make the Manchego wafers. In a small bowl, mix together the cheese, paprika and thyme. Line two large baking trays with baking paper. Allowing six wafers per baking tray, and 1 level tablespoon of cheese mixture per wafer, scoop the mixture onto the trays, spacing them well apart. Spread them into flat disc shapes about 8 cm (3¹/₄ inch) in diameter — if you like, use an 8 cm (3¹/₄ inch) biscuit (cookie) cutter as a guide. Bake for 4–5 minutes, or until golden and bubbling. Remove from the oven and set aside. They will become crisp on sitting.

Turn the oven temperature down to 160°C (315°F/Gas 2–3). Cut the eggplant in half down the middle and scoop the flesh out into a food processor, discarding any skin. Peel the capsicum, onion and garlic, roughly chop the flesh and add to the food processor. Blend until finely chopped. Add the egg yolks, cream and thyme, season with a little freshly ground black pepper, then blend until just smooth — do not overblend or the cream will split.

Pour into six 125 ml (4 fl oz/¹/₂ cup) lightly oiled ramekins or ovenproof glasses, but do not fill them all the way to the top. Put the moulds in a baking tray, then pour enough water into the tray to come halfway up the sides. Bake for 50 minutes to 1 hour, or until the custards are firm to the touch. Lift them out of their water bath, leave to rest for 10 minutes, then serve with two Manchego wafers per person. To serve cold, refrigerate for about 4 hours before serving.

Named after the barbed bullfighters' sticks, *banderilla* are small skewers holding just
a few delicious morsels of food. Try experimenting with sliced chorizo, artichokes,
pickled baby onions, olives, cheese, prawns (shrimp) — whatever takes your fancy.

tuna banderilla with lemon dressing

lemon dressing
1 1/2 tablespoons lemon juice
2 tablespoons extra virgin olive oil
1/2 teaspoon dijon mustard
1/2 teaspoon thyme leaves
pinch of caster (superfine) sugar

600 g (1 lb 5 oz) sashimi-grade tuna, cut into 3 cm
    (1 1/4 inch) cubes (you will need 24 pieces in total)
olive oil, for pan-frying
6 cooked white asparagus spears (either fresh or
    bottled), each cut into 3 lengths
12 small caperberries
4 guindilla chillies in vinegar, each cut into 3 lengths

Makes 12

If you don't have 12 short metal skewers, soak 12 short wooden skewers
in cold water for 2 hours to prevent scorching.

Meanwhile, make the lemon dressing. Whisk together the lemon juice, oil,
mustard, thyme and a pinch of sugar until well blended. Season to taste,
then set aside to allow the flavours to develop.

Lightly season the tuna cubes. Brush a large frying pan with oil and place
over high heat. Sear the tuna cubes in two batches for about 20 seconds
on each side, then remove from the pan.

Thread two alternating pieces of asparagus and tuna onto a skewer, then
finish off with a caperberry and a piece of chilli. Repeat with all the remaining
ingredients to make 12 skewers.

Whisk the lemon dressing again, stack the skewers on a serving plate, drizzle
the dressing over and serve.

Mussel shells make superb little platters for dishing up finger food. Here the shells are filled with chopped, steamed mussels in a thick, spicy tomato sauce, served warm beneath a crunchy cheese topping.

chilli mussels

chilli tomato sauce
2 tablespoons olive oil
$1/2$ red onion, finely chopped
3 garlic cloves, crushed
1–2 small red chillies, seeded and very finely chopped
$1/4$ teaspoon smoked sweet paprika
24 mussels, scrubbed and bearded
60 ml (2 fl oz/$1/4$ cup) white wine
60 ml (2 fl oz/$1/4$ cup) fino (dry) sherry
125 g ($4^1/2$ oz/$1/2$ cup) crushed tinned tomatoes
1 teaspoon finely chopped thyme
1 teaspoon caster (superfine) sugar

topping
30 g (1 oz/$1/3$ cup) finely grated Manchego cheese
55 g (2 oz/$2/3$ cup) breadcrumbs, made from
  day-old bread
$1^1/2$ tablespoons flat-leaf (Italian) parsley, finely chopped
olive oil, for drizzling

Makes 24

First, make the chilli tomato sauce. Heat the oil in a large saucepan over medium heat, then add the onion and cook, stirring, for 5 minutes, or until soft and golden. Add the garlic, chilli and paprika and cook for a further 30 seconds, or until fragrant. Increase the heat to high and add the mussels, wine, sherry and a large pinch of salt. Stir everything together, then cover and cook, shaking the pan occasionally, for 3–4 minutes, or until the mussels pop open. Discard any that remain closed. Remove the mussels from the pan and leave until cool enough to handle.

While the mussels are cooling, stir the crushed tomatoes into the sauce along with the thyme, sugar and 125 ml (4 fl oz/$1/2$ cup) of water. Bring to the boil and allow to boil for 15 minutes, stirring regularly, until thick and pulpy — you should have about 185 ml (6 fl oz/$3/4$ cup) of sauce.

Meanwhile, when the mussels are cool enough to handle, pull them out of their shells and set aside. Pull the shells apart at their hinges into two halves. Choose the 24 biggest halves, remove any muscle with a sharp knife, then rinse well and pat dry with paper towels. Discard the remaining shells.

Finely chop the mussel meat, stir it through the sauce, then take the sauce off the heat. Spoon the sauce into the mussel shells and sit them on a foil-lined baking tray.

Preheat the grill (broiler) to high. To make the topping, combine the cheese, breadcrumbs and parsley and sprinkle it over the mussels. Drizzle with olive oil, then put the baking tray under the grill and cook for 2–3 minutes, or until the topping is crisp and golden. Serve at once.

Morcilla, a rich, lightly spiced Spanish blood sausage similar to black pudding, is often simply served sliced on bread. If you find it too rich, try this version, shot with the sharp, sweet flavours of apples in various guises — the fruit, cider and cider vinegar.

pan-fried morcilla with apples and sage

20 g (³/4 oz) butter

2 teaspoons olive oil

12 sage leaves

1 fuji or pink lady apple, cut into thin wedges and cored

250 g (9 oz) morcilla sausages or black pudding, cut into 8 mm (³/8 inch) thick slices

80 ml (2¹/2 fl oz/¹/3 cup) dry Spanish *sidra,* or other dry alcoholic apple cider

2 tablespoons cider vinegar

Serves 4–6

Melt the butter and oil in a large frying pan over medium–high heat. Add the sage leaves and cook, stirring, for 1¹/2 minutes, or until fragrant and crispy. Remove and drain on crumpled paper towels. Add the apple to the pan and sauté for 2 minutes, or until lightly golden but still quite crisp. Remove from the pan and set aside.

Sear the sausage slices in the same pan for 20 seconds on each side. Increase the heat to high, pour in the cider and cider vinegar and cook for 1–2 minutes, or until the liquid has evaporated.

Take the pan off the heat and crumble half the sage leaves over the top. Season to taste, then gently stir the apple through — the sausage crumbles easily so don't overmix. Serve at once, garnished with the remaining sage.

Variation: Instead of mixing the sautéed apple through the sausages, you could serve a slice of the cooked morcilla on a slice of crisp raw apple, topped with a sage leaf. You will need 2–3 sliced apples if you are serving the dish in this way.

Many tapas items tend to be on the rich and spicy side, so this fresh green salad with cooling avocado is a great addition to any tapas table. The dressing is based on the summery Spanish tomato soup, gazpacho.

avocado salad with gazpacho dressing

gazpacho dressing
$1/2$ red capsicum (pepper)
$1/2$ Lebanese (short) cucumber
1 large ripe tomato, seeded
2 garlic cloves
2 teaspoons sherry vinegar
60 ml (2 fl oz/$1/4$ cup) extra virgin olive oil
large pinch of caster (superfine) sugar

2 ripe avocados
100 g ($3^1/2$ oz/4 cups) mixed green leaves, such as
    baby rocket (arugula), flat-leaf (Italian) parsley,
    witlof (chicory/Belgian endive), frisée (curly endive),
    baby English spinach or baby cos (romaine) lettuce

Serves 8

First, make the gazpacho dressing. Chop the capsicum, cucumber, tomato and garlic and place in a food processor. Blend until smooth, then strain into a bowl, pressing on the solids to release as much liquid as possible. Discard the solids. Add the sherry vinegar, oil and sugar and whisk until the sugar has dissolved. Season to taste, then cover and refrigerate for 30 minutes.

Just before serving, cut each avocado in half and carefully remove the stone. Using a large spoon, scoop the avocado halves out of their skins. Slice each avocado portion in half lengthways to give eight avocado quarters.

Arrange the salad leaves on a platter with the avocado. Whisk the dressing again, drizzle over the salad, sprinkle with freshly cracked black pepper and serve. Alternatively, divide the leaves among eight small plates, arrange an avocado slice on top, drizzle with dressing, sprinkle with pepper and serve.

Most of us know *tortilla* as a Spanish potato omelette served hot or cold in thick wedges. Tender flakes of salt cod bring a new dimension to these individual treats, which are perfect for picnics and cocktail parties. The browned lemon butter is optional.

mini salt cod tortillas

200 g (7 oz) bacalao (dried salt cod)
1 fresh bay leaf
1 large all-purpose potato (about 200 g/7 oz)
1¹/₂ tablespoons olive oil, plus extra for brushing
¹/₂ small red onion, very finely chopped
2 garlic cloves, crushed
3 large eggs
1 tablespoon finely chopped flat-leaf (Italian) parsley
lemon wedges, to serve

browned lemon butter
40 g (1¹/₂ oz) butter
¹/₂ teaspoon finely grated lemon zest
1 teaspoon lemon juice

Makes 24

Soak the cod in cold water in the refrigerator for 24 hours, changing the water several times. Drain well, then place in a saucepan of water with the bay leaf. Bring to the boil, then reduce the heat and simmer for 25 minutes, or until the fish flakes easily. Drain the liquid and discard the bay leaf. Remove any skin and bones from the fish, then finely flake the flesh with a fork.

Meanwhile, peel the potato, cut it into quarters and cook in boiling water for 10 minutes, or until tender. Drain and set aside until cool enough to handle, then cut into 5 mm (¹/₄ inch) cubes. Heat the oil in a frying pan over medium–high heat, then add the onion and cook, stirring, for 8–10 minutes, or until lightly golden. Add the garlic and potato cubes and fry for 1 minute, then set aside to cool.

Preheat the oven to 160°C (315°F/Gas 2–3). In a bowl, lightly beat the eggs, then add the cod flakes, potato mixture and parsley. Stir to combine and season well. Divide the mixture among 24 oiled, non-stick mini-muffin holes, but don't fill them right up to the top. Bake for 7–8 minutes, or until just set. Remove from the oven, rest for a few minutes, then carefully turn the *tortillas* onto a serving plate while still warm. Serve at once, with lemon wedges.

If making the browned lemon butter, start while the *tortillas* are baking. Put the butter in a saucepan over low–medium heat with the lemon zest and cook for 3 minutes, or until the butter foams and subsides. Reduce the heat to low and cook for 3–4 minutes, or until the butter turns nut brown and has a toasty aroma. Immediately take the pan off the heat and add the lemon juice. Drizzle over the warm *tortillas*, or serve as a dipping sauce.

These sexy sippers feature three iconic Spanish ingredients: grapes, almonds and coffee. Traditionally, *horchata* does not include alcohol so feel free to omit the sherry and liqueur for a refreshing summer drink — or serve with a small spoon for a light summer dessert.

green grape martini

500 g (1 lb 2 oz) seedless green grapes, chilled
170 ml (5^1/$_2$ fl oz/^{2}/$_3$ cup) gin, chilled
170 ml (5^1/$_2$ fl oz/^{2}/$_3$ cup) fino (dry) sherry, chilled
12 green grapes, extra, to garnish

Serves 6

Juice the grapes using a juice extractor or food processor, or purée them in a blender. Strain the liquid through a very fine sieve into a pitcher. Pour in the gin and sherry and stir, then pour into six chilled martini glasses. Thread two grapes onto six toothpicks or short skewers and use them to garnish each martini.

frosted horchata

250 g (9 oz/1^2/$_3$ cups) blanched almonds
^{1}/$_4$ lemon, chopped but not peeled
1 cinnamon stick
115 g (4 oz/^{1}/$_2$ cup) caster (superfine) sugar
1 tablespoon Pedro Ximénez sherry
1^1/$_2$ tablespoons fino (dry) sherry
2 tablespoons almond liqueur, such as amaretto

Serves 6

Finely grind the almonds in a food processor. With the motor still running, gradually add 375 ml (13 fl oz/1^1/$_2$ cups) of boiling water. Pour into a non-metallic bowl and add the lemon, cinnamon stick, sugar and another 500 ml (17 fl oz/2 cups) of boiling water. Stir well, then leave at room temperature for 3 hours, stirring occasionally.

Strain through muslin (cheese cloth) or a tea towel (dish towel), squeezing out any liquid. Pour into two or three ice-cube trays and freeze for 5 hours.

When you're nearly ready to serve, take the *horchata* ice cubes out of the freezer and leave for 10 minutes. Combine the sherries and the liqueur. In two batches, process the ice cubes and liqueur mixture in a blender until finely crushed and slushy. Pour into six glasses and serve at once.

cinnamon, coffee and vanilla-infused vodka

2 cinnamon sticks
1 vanilla bean, split and cut into thirds
3 teaspoons fresh coffee beans
750 ml (26 fl oz) bottle good-quality vodka

Makes 1 x 750 ml (26 fl oz) bottle

Put the cinnamon sticks, vanilla bean, coffee beans and 80 ml (2^1/$_2$ fl oz/^{1}/$_3$ cup) of the vodka in a small saucepan over low heat for 2–3 minutes, or until a few bubbles rise to the surface. Leave to cool to room temperature, then lift out the solids, return them to the vodka bottle and pour in the warmed vodka. Close the lid tightly and shake. Allow to infuse for 2 days, shaking the bottle occasionally — the longer it sits, the stronger the flavour. If it becomes too strong, dilute with fresh vodka. Store the bottle in the freezer and use in martinis, mixed drinks or topped up with soda, or even cola for a super caffeine boost.

Delectable duck, marinated overnight and very slowly cooked in its own flavoursome fat with plenty of garlic, bay leaves, fennel seeds and cumin, is so very silky and delicious that it's worth every minute of the lengthy preparation time for this dish.

spanish-style duck rillette

4 duck leg quarters (about 220 g/7³/4 oz each)
1¹/2 tablespoons rock salt
3 garlic cloves, chopped
3 fresh bay leaves, torn
3 tablespoons fennel seeds, toasted and lightly crushed
2 tablespoons cumin seeds, toasted and lightly crushed
2 tablespoons finely chopped thyme
3 x 350 g (12 oz) tins duck fat
1 large thyme sprig
4 garlic cloves, extra, finely chopped
¹/2 teaspoon finely chopped thyme, extra
1 fresh bay leaf, extra, to garnish

Serves 8–10

Sit the duck in a large non-metallic dish. Combine the rock salt, garlic, torn bay leaves, fennel seeds, cumin seeds and thyme, then rub the mixture all over the duck. Cover the dish tightly with several layers of plastic wrap and refrigerate for 24 hours.

Lightly rinse the duck and pat dry with paper towels. Put the duck fat in a large, deep, heavy-based saucepan, then push the duck legs into the fat, making sure they are well covered. Add the thyme sprig and the extra garlic. Put the pan over medium–high heat and allow to just come to the boil, then reduce the heat to low and cook slowly for 4 hours, or until the meat falls off the bone easily.

Take the pan off the heat and allow to cool a little. When the duck is cool enough to handle, lift it all out, reserving the fat. Pull off the skin and discard, then remove the meat from the bones and place on a chopping board. Using one fork to hold the meat in place, use a second fork to pull and shred the duck meat into very fine, hairy strands. Combine with 185 ml (6 fl oz/³/4 cup) of the reserved fat and the extra chopped thyme and season to taste.

Pack the shredded duck mixture into a 750 ml (26 fl oz/3 cup) non-metallic serving dish and smooth the top. Press the whole bay leaf into the centre, then pour over enough of the reserved fat to cover the top by about 3 mm (¹/8 inch). Tap the dish on the bench to remove any air bubbles, and top up with a little more fat if necessary to ensure the surface remains completely covered. Refrigerate for 3 hours, or until the fat firms a little and turns opaque again. Serve with toasts, sticky muscatels (see page 32), and guindilla chillies in vinegar. Lovely with a glass of oloroso sherry.

Note: The rillette will keep for several weeks in the refrigerator provided it is completely covered with the fat. If you only need enough for 4–6 people, divide the mixture between two serving dishes and keep one in the refrigerator for another occasion — if you can refrain from eating it yourself. Strain any remaining fat through a very fine sieve and refrigerate for up to 2 months — you can use it for making the crispy duck with fennel salad on page 138, or for cooking the best roast potatoes in the world!

Curiously, Russian salad is found all over Spain. It is a popular tapas item featuring a variety of vegetables and home-made mayonnaise. With a touch of dill it becomes the perfect partner for seafood, especially shellfish such as lobster or prawns.

lobster russian salad

1 small carrot, finely diced (about pea size)
40 g (1¹/₂ oz/¹/₄ cup) frozen peas
2 artichoke hearts in oil, drained and finely diced
1 tablespoon finely diced *pimientos del piquillo*
3 teaspoons lemon juice
125 g (4¹/₂ oz/¹/₂ cup) mayonnaise (see Basics, page 187)
large pinch of caster (superfine) sugar
2 teaspoons finely chopped dill
2 teaspoons very finely chopped red onion
dash of dry anis, or other dry aniseed liqueur
2 small cooked lobster tails, or 500 g (1 lb 2 oz) cooked
    king prawns (shrimp), peeled and deveined
black caviar or fish roe (optional), to garnish

Serves 6

Bring a saucepan of water to the boil. Add the carrot and cook for 3 minutes, or until tender. Remove with a slotted spoon, drain well and place in a bowl. Cook the peas in the same pan for 1 minute, or until tender. Remove with a slotted spoon, drain well, then add to the carrots with the artichoke, pimiento, lemon juice, mayonnaise, sugar, dill, onion and anis. Mix well and season to taste.

Remove the meat from the lobster tails, slice it in half lengthways, then cut into small neat chunks. Divide among six small, squat glasses and top with the salad mixture. Garnish with caviar (if using) and serve at once, with small forks.

Almost like compact paellas, these flavoursome little cakes are delicious on their own with a glass of Spanish red, or shaped into six larger cakes and topped with grilled seafood or meats. For a more substantial meal, just add a crisp green salad.

saffron rice cakes

1–1.5 litres (35–52 fl oz/4–6 cups) home-made or
    low-salt chicken stock
olive oil, for pan-frying
1 red onion, finely chopped
3 garlic cloves, very finely chopped
3 slices jamón, prosciutto or jambon, finely chopped
1/4 teaspoon smoked paprika
1/4 teaspoon sweet paprika
pinch of saffron threads
330 g (11 1/2 oz/1 1/2 cups) Calasparra or paella rice
1 tablespoon tomato paste (concentrated purée)
60 ml (2 fl oz/1/4 cup) fino (dry) sherry
6 pitted black olives, finely chopped
2 *pimientos del piquillo*, finely chopped
2 tablespoons finely chopped flat-leaf (Italian) parsley
50 g (1 3/4 oz/1/2 cup) grated Manchego cheese
plain (all-purpose) flour, for coating
lemon wedges (optional), to serve
mayonnaise (optional), to serve (see Basics, page 187)

Makes 18

Bring the stock to the boil over high heat, then immediately reduce the heat to a very gentle simmer.

Heat 2 tablespoons of olive oil in a large saucepan over medium heat. Add the onion and cook for 6–8 minutes, stirring occasionally, until lightly golden. Stir in the garlic, jamón, smoked and sweet paprika and saffron and cook for 1 minute. Add the rice and stir for 2 minutes, or until the grains are well coated and a little opaque. Stir in the tomato paste and sherry and cook for 1 minute, then add 125 ml (4 fl oz/1/2 cup) of the hot stock and stir until it is completely absorbed into the rice. Keep adding the stock, 125 ml (4 fl oz/1/2 cup) at a time, stirring constantly, until all the stock has been absorbed and the rice is tender — this should take about 25 minutes.

Let the rice cool slightly, then stir in the olives, pimiento, parsley and cheese. Season to taste, then empty into a bowl. Allow to cool a little more, then cover and refrigerate for 2 1/2–3 hours, or until completely cold.

Taking about 2 tablespoons at a time, form the rice mixture into 18 patties. Pour enough oil into a large non-stick frying pan to cover the base by 2 mm (1/16 inch) and place over medium heat. Lightly coat the rice cakes with flour, then cook in three batches for 5 minutes on each side, or until crisp, golden and heated through. Serve with lemon wedges, or a dollop of mayonnaise.

Note: This recipe also makes a great risotto for four. As soon as you have finished adding all the stock, stir in the olives, pimiento, parsley and cheese and serve immediately, perhaps scattered with some sautéed chorizo slices.

A nice change from heavier creamy potato salads, this warm salad of tender potato slices and crispy chorizo is lightly coated with a fresh, zippy mint dressing. The mint is a cool complement to the rich spiciness of the chorizo.

warm chorizo, potato and mint salad

mint dressing
1¹/2 tablespoons sherry vinegar
2 teaspoons lemon juice
1 garlic clove, crushed
1 teaspoon dijon mustard
large pinch of sugar
60 ml (2 fl oz/¹/4 cup) extra virgin olive oil
1 large handful mint, finely shredded

500 g (1 lb 2 oz) waxy potatoes, such as kipfler
    (fingerling), washed but not peeled, sliced 2 cm
    (³/4 inch) thick
1 chorizo sausage, cut into 1 cm (¹/2 inch) cubes

Serves 4–6

First, make the mint dressing. Mix the vinegar, lemon juice, garlic, mustard and sugar together in a small bowl, then whisk in the oil. Stir in the mint and set aside for the flavours to infuse.

Cook the potato slices in a saucepan of salted boiling water for 12 minutes, or until tender. Drain well.

While the potato is cooking, put a lightly oiled frying pan over medium–high heat and cook the chorizo for 10 minutes, or until crispy, stirring now and then. Remove and drain on crumpled paper towels.

Put the chorizo in a serving bowl with the warm potato and the dressing. Toss together gently, then season to taste and serve.

Lentils aren't normally thought of as tapas fare, but this gorgeous little stew starring very tender, slow-cooked baby squid is worthy of any tapas table. Deliciously heady with saffron and red wine, this dish is very rich, so a little goes a long way.

baby squid with sweet onion and lentils

60 ml (2 fl oz/¼ cup) olive oil
2 red onions, thinly sliced
1 small celery stalk, very finely diced
1 fresh bay leaf
400 g (14 oz) cleaned whole baby squid
2 large ripe tomatoes, peeled, seeded and chopped
pinch of saffron threads
310 ml (10¾ fl oz/1¼ cups) home-made or
    low-salt fish stock
170 ml (5½ fl oz/⅔ cup) red wine
1 strip of lemon zest
1 teaspoon soft brown sugar
½ teaspoon finely chopped thyme
100 g (3½ oz/½ cup) puy lentils or tiny
    blue-green lentils
flat-leaf (Italian) parsley, to garnish
lemon wedges, to serve
allioli, to serve (see Basics, page 187)

Serves 4–6

Put the oil in a large saucepan over medium–low heat. Add the onion, celery, bay leaf and a large pinch of salt and cook gently for 20 minutes, or until the vegetables are just starting to stick a little during stirring. Reduce the heat to low and cook for another 1 hour and 10 minutes, stirring frequently, until the onion is soft and deep golden. Don't rush this step — the onion needs to cook slowly to ensure it caramelizes well without burning.

When the onion has finished caramelizing, add the squid, tomato, saffron, stock, wine, lemon zest, sugar and thyme. Increase the heat to high, bring to the boil, then reduce the heat and simmer for 1½–2 hours, or until the squid is very tender and the sauce has thickened.

When the squid is nearly cooked, rinse the lentils, then cook them in a saucepan of boiling water for 10–12 minutes, or until tender but not too soft. (Alternatively, cook them according to the packet instructions.) Drain well, then stir them through the squid mixture and cook for a few more minutes to heat through. Season to taste, garnish with parsley and serve at once, with lemon wedges and a little allioli on the side.

Spanish markets carry a vast array of exotic, freshly picked mushrooms. An aromatic plateful gently sautéed with golden garlic is a fine treat indeed, but add some herbs and a decadent drizzle of truffle oil and you have magic mushrooms of the legal kind.

sautéed mixed mushrooms with garlic

400 g (14 oz) mixed fresh mushrooms,
    the finest of the season
60 g (2¼ oz) butter
2 tablespoons extra virgin olive oil
6 garlic cloves, finely chopped
2 tablespoons fino (dry) sherry
1½ teaspoons sherry vinegar
1½ teaspoons chopped oregano
2 tablespoons chopped flat-leaf (Italian) parsley
black truffle oil (optional), for drizzling
tiny whole oregano leaves, extra, to garnish

Serves 4–6

Check the mushrooms are free from grit, then trim the stems. Slice any large mushrooms, and either keep the small ones whole or cut them in half.

Put the butter and oil in a large frying pan over medium–low heat. When the butter has melted, add the garlic and cook, stirring, for 4–5 minutes, or until golden, making sure it doesn't burn.

Add the mushrooms and a pinch of salt and sauté for 4 minutes, or until they start to soften. Increase the heat to high and add the sherry, sherry vinegar and chopped oregano. Sauté for a further 4–5 minutes, or until most of the liquid has evaporated. Season to taste with salt and freshly cracked black pepper, then stir the parsley through.

Put the mushrooms in a serving dish, drizzle with truffle oil (if using), sprinkle with a few whole oregano leaves and serve.

In this attractive dish, chicken breasts are rolled around a delicious mixture of spinach, raisins and pine nuts, lightly spiced with cinnamon. They are then bound up with melty Manchego and deep fried, rendering the chicken succulent and tender.

pollo rollo

filling
20 g ($^3/_4$ oz) butter
2 tablespoons pine nuts
2 garlic cloves, crushed
$^1/_4$ teaspoon ground cinnamon
135 g ($4^3/_4$ oz/3 cups) baby English spinach leaves
2 tablespoons raisins, chopped
80 g ($2^3/_4$ oz/$^3/_4$ cup) grated Manchego cheese
2 teaspoons lemon juice

3 large boneless, skinless chicken breasts
    (about 250 g/9 oz each)
plain (all-purpose) flour, for coating
2 eggs, lightly beaten
seasoned dry breadcrumbs, for coating
olive oil, for deep-frying

Makes about 18 pieces

First, make the filling. Melt the butter in a frying pan over medium heat. Add the pine nuts and cook for 1–2 minutes, or until pale golden. Stir in the garlic and cinnamon and cook for 30 seconds, or until fragrant. Add the spinach and toss until wilted, then remove from the heat, add the raisins and leave to cool. When the mixture has cooled, stir in the cheese and lemon juice, mix well and season to taste.

Lay the chicken breasts flat on a chopping board with the pointed end towards you. Using a very sharp knife, make a cut down into the breast, as if you're about to make two smaller breasts, but stopping about 5 mm ($^1/_4$ inch) before you go right through. At that point, using a smooth but slight sawing action, cut to the left, gently and slowly pulling the flesh out to the left as you go — you should end up with one 5 mm ($^1/_4$ inch) thick flap, like a thin schnitzel. Repeat on the right-hand side to make one big, schnitzel-like piece of chicken. Repeat with the other two chicken breasts.

Place a third of the filling over each breast, leaving a bit of a border around the edges, and press down with your hands to evenly flatten them. Roll each piece up into a log, then cover firmly with plastic wrap and twist the ends of the plastic to form a neat bon-bon shape. Refrigerate for at least 1 hour.

Unwrap the chicken and lightly coat with flour. Dip each log in the beaten egg, allowing any excess to drip off, then roll them in the breadcrumbs, pressing the crumbs in to help them stick — make sure the rolls are well covered. Refrigerate for 30 minutes.

Fill a deep-fryer or large heavy-based saucepan one-third full of oil and heat to 170°C (325°F), or until a cube of bread dropped into the oil browns in 20 seconds. Add the chicken, one roll at a time, and cook for 10 minutes, or until the coating is deep golden and the chicken is cooked all the way through. Drain on crumpled paper towels and keep warm in a very low oven while cooking the remaining rolls. Allow the chicken to rest for a few minutes, then trim the ends off and cut each roll on the diagonal into 1.5 cm ($^5/_8$ inch) thick slices. Serve immediately.

A wonderful tapas of pork belly slowly cooked in home-made almond milk. The meat melts in the mouth, and the silky, creamy almond sauce is worthy of sipping in little cups alongside the pork, perhaps with a blissful dash of almond-flavoured liqueur.

pork belly in almond milk

1 kg (2 lb 4 oz) piece of boneless pork belly
1 tablespoon sugar
1 tablespoon finely chopped thyme
4 garlic cloves, finely chopped
2 fresh bay leaves, torn into small pieces
large pinch of freshly ground white pepper
1 tablespoon salt
1 litre (35 fl oz/4 cups) home-made or low-salt
   chicken stock
amaretto or other almond-flavoured liqueur (optional),
   to taste

almond milk
250 g (9 oz/1²/₃ cups) blanched almonds
500 ml (17 fl oz/2 cups) milk
375 ml (13 fl oz/1¹/₂ cups) cream (whipping)
1 large strip of lemon zest

aromatic sprinkle
1¹/₂ teaspoons finely chopped thyme
2 teaspoons finely grated lemon zest
1 teaspoon ground cinnamon

Makes 12 pieces

Put the pork belly in a non-metallic baking dish. In a small bowl, mix together the sugar, thyme, garlic, bay leaves, white pepper and salt. Rub the mixture thoroughly all over the pork, then cover with plastic wrap. Weigh the pork down with a slightly smaller baking dish filled with water to keep it flat. Refrigerate for 24 hours.

Rinse the pork well and pat dry. Sit it in a large saucepan, then pour in the stock and 1 litre (35 fl oz/4 cups) of water. Bring to the boil, then reduce the heat and simmer, turning the pork occasionally, for 1¹/₂ hours, or until it is starting to become tender.

Meanwhile, make the almond milk. Finely grind the almonds in a food processor, then transfer to a saucepan with the milk, cream and lemon zest. Bring to the boil and allow to boil for 5 minutes to infuse the flavours, then remove from the heat and allow to come to room temperature. Strain into a large, clean saucepan.

Remove the pork from the stock and put it in the saucepan, rind side up, with the almond milk. Strain the stock over the pork and stir gently to combine. Bring to the boil, then reduce the heat, cover and simmer for 1¹/₄ hours, or until very tender. Lift the pork out of the sauce, cover to keep warm and set aside. Bring the sauce back to the boil and cook for 45 minutes, or until the sauce has reduced and thickened.

Slice the pork into 12 rectangular portions, about 4 x 6 cm (1¹/₂–2¹/₂ inches) in size. In a small bowl, mix together the aromatic sprinkle ingredients.

Place the pork on small individual plates and sprinkle with the spice mix. Serve the sauce — with a dash of amaretto if desired — either drizzled over the pork, in shot glasses on the side, or as a separate tapas of almond soup.

cocina

Based on a rich, golden, home-made chicken stock, this wonderful lemon-scented broth contains delicious tiny chicken meatballs, sweet tender vegetables and wholesome chickpeas.

chicken broth with chickpeas and sherry

chicken stock
2 tablespoons olive oil
2 kg (4 lb 8 oz) chicken bones
1 large brown onion, chopped
1 large carrot, chopped
1 celery stalk, plus a few celery leaves, chopped
2 garlic cloves, bruised
1 fresh bay leaf
3 parsley stems (without leaves), chopped
1 large thyme sprig

1 quantity of chicken meatball mixture from page 59
2 carrots, cut into 1 cm (1/2 inch) cubes
2 celery stalks, cut into 1 cm (1/2 inch) cubes
400 g (14 oz) tin chickpeas
1/2 teaspoon finely grated lemon zest
1 teaspoon finely chopped thyme
small pinch of saffron
60 ml (2 fl oz/1/4 cup) manzanilla sherry
2 tablespoons lemon juice
flat-leaf (Italian) parsley leaves, to serve

Serves 4–6 as a light meal

Start by making the chicken stock. Heat the oil in a stockpot or very large saucepan over medium heat. Brown the chicken bones in two batches for 8 minutes each time, or until golden, then remove. Cook the onion, carrot and celery stalk in the same pot for 10 minutes, or until golden, stirring now and then. Put the chicken bones back in the pot, along with the celery leaves, garlic, bay leaf, parsley stems, thyme and 4 litres (140 fl oz/16 cups) of cold water. Increase the heat to high, bring to the boil, then reduce the heat and simmer for 3 hours, or until the broth has a rich chicken flavour, removing any scum that forms on the surface during cooking.

While the stock is simmering, form heaped teaspoons of the chicken mixture into mini meatballs and refrigerate until ready to use.

Strain the chicken stock into a large saucepan, pressing on the solids to release as much liquid as possible. Bring to the boil again, then reduce to a simmer. Add the carrot, celery, chickpeas, lemon zest, thyme, saffron and sherry. Cook for 5–6 minutes, or until the vegetables are just tender.

Add the chicken meatballs and allow the stock to come to the boil again — by this stage all the meatballs should have risen to the surface and be cooked through. Take the soup off the heat, stir in the lemon juice and season to taste. Serve at once, garnished with a few parsley leaves.

Note: For a more substantial meal, add some cooked rice or vermicelli noodles in the final stages of cooking.

This is a simple, fresh risotto using Spanish paella rice instead of risotto rice, resulting in a slightly less creamy texture. The jamón, sherry and Manchego cheese replace traditional Italian ingredients such as prosciutto, white wine and parmesan.

jamón and greens risotto

500 g (1 lb 2 oz) fresh broad (fava) beans in the pod
(see Note)
300 g (10^1/$_2$ oz) fresh peas in the pod (see Note)
175 g (6 oz/1 bunch) thin asparagus, cut into 3 cm
(1^1/$_4$ inch) lengths
1.25 litres (44 fl oz/5 cups) home-made or low-salt
chicken stock, or vegetable stock
1 tablespoon olive oil
40 g (1^1/$_2$ oz) butter
1 leek, white part only, chopped
1 fresh bay leaf
3 garlic cloves, finely chopped
100 g (3^1/$_2$ oz) jamón, prosciutto or jambon, finely sliced
1 teaspoon finely chopped thyme
440 g (15^1/$_2$ oz/2 cups) Calasparra or paella rice
125 ml (4 fl oz/^{1}/$_2$ cup) fino (dry) sherry
100 g (3^1/$_2$ oz/2^1/$_4$ cups) baby English spinach leaves
80 g (2^3/$_4$ oz/^{3}/$_4$ cup) grated Manchego cheese,
plus extra, for sprinkling

Serves 4–6

Shell the broad beans and peas. Bring a small saucepan of water to the boil. Add the broad beans and cook for 3 minutes, or until just tender, then scoop out with a slotted spoon and plunge into a bowl of cold water. Cook the peas in the same water for 2 minutes, or until just tender, then scoop them out and add to the broad beans. Cook the asparagus in the same water for 1 minute, then scoop out and add to the broad beans. Strain and reserve 375 ml (13 fl oz/1^1/$_2$ cups) of the cooking liquid. When the vegetables are cool enough to handle, drain them well, then slip the beans out of their skins. Set aside.

Pour the stock and reserved vegetable cooking liquid into a saucepan, bring to the boil, then reduce the heat to a low simmer.

Heat the oil and butter in a large saucepan over medium heat. Add the leek and bay leaf and cook, stirring occasionally, for 3 minutes, or until the leek has softened and is lightly golden. Add the garlic, jamón and thyme and cook for 1 minute, or until fragrant. Add the rice and stir to coat. Cook for 2–3 minutes, or until the rice is slightly translucent.

Increase the heat to high, add the sherry and stir until it has all been absorbed. Add 125 ml (4 fl oz/^{1}/$_2$ cup) of the simmering stock, stirring until absorbed. Stirring constantly, continue adding the stock in this way, until it is nearly used up. With the last 125 ml (4 fl oz/^{1}/$_2$ cup) of stock, add the spinach, broad beans, peas and asparagus to heat through — the rice should be tender but not mushy. Stir the cheese through, season to taste and serve at once, with extra grated cheese on the side for sprinkling over.

Note: If broad (fava) beans are out of season, you could instead use 165 g (5^3/$_4$ oz/1 cup) of frozen broad beans. If fresh peas are not available, use 115 g (4 oz/^{3}/$_4$ cup) of frozen peas.

Traditionally, *marmitako* is a type of fish and vegetable stew. This baked version of the Spanish classic is attractively presented in parcels that are opened at the table, unleashing a host of appetizing aromas.

marmitako parcels

2 large all-purpose potatoes, such as desiree or
    pontiac (about 450 g/1 lb in total)
1 green capsicum (pepper), cut in half
1 large zucchini (courgette), cut in half, then thinly
    sliced lengthways
80 ml (2^{1}/$_{2}$ fl oz/^{1}/$_{3}$ cup) extra virgin olive oil
3 garlic cloves, crushed
2 teaspoons finely chopped thyme
1 teaspoon finely grated lemon zest
^{1}/$_{2}$ small red onion, very thinly sliced
2 ripe tomatoes, thinly sliced
4 x 220 g (7^{3}/$_{4}$ oz) blue eye cod fillets, or other
    firm white fish fillets
4 small thyme sprigs, extra, to garnish
lemon wedges, to serve

Serves 4

Peel the potatoes and slice them very thinly using a mandolin — or a very sharp knife and a steady hand!

Bring a large saucepan of salted water to the boil. Add the potato slices and cook for 2 minutes, or until just tender. Drain well and rinse with cold water, then spread out to dry in a single layer on a clean tea towel (dish towel) or paper towels.

Preheat the grill (broiler) to high. Cook the capsicum, skin side up, under the hot grill for about 10 minutes, or until the skin blackens and blisters. Leave to cool in a plastic bag, then peel away the skin and cut the flesh into wide strips.

While the capsicum is sweating, brush the zucchini with some of the oil, sprinkle with salt and grill (broil) for 8 minutes, or until golden.

Preheat the oven to 190°C (375°F/Gas 5). Combine the remaining oil with the garlic, thyme and lemon zest. Take a large piece of baking paper and overlap a quarter of the potato slices along the middle. Drizzle with some of the garlic oil mixture and sprinkle with salt. Arrange a quarter of the capsicum, onion, tomato and zucchini slices over the top, then drizzle with a little more of the oil and sprinkle again with salt. Top with a fish fillet and garnish with a sprig of thyme. Fold the paper over, then roll up the edges to form a neat, sealed packet (you can even staple the edges together if you like). Repeat to make four parcels.

Put the parcels on a baking tray and bake for 20 minutes, or until the fish is opaque and flakes easily when tested with a fork — the exact cooking time will vary depending on the thickness of the fish. Put the parcels on four serving plates and allow your guests to open them at the table. Serve with lemon wedges for squeezing over.

This unusual dish of slow-cooked lamb in creamy sheep's yoghurt just melts in the mouth. Aromatic with cinnamon, lemon and herbs, it is a play on the divine Italian dish of pork cooked in milk, *maiale al latte*.

lamb in sheep's yoghurt

60 ml (2 fl oz/¼ cup) olive oil
1 large brown onion, thinly sliced
3 garlic cloves, finely chopped
12 lamb leg or shoulder chops, each about
    1.5–2 cm (⁵⁄₈–³⁄₄ inch) thick
1 large rosemary sprig
1 large oregano sprig
1 large thyme sprig
2 large mint sprigs
375 g (13 oz/1½ cups) sheep's milk yoghurt
375 ml (13 fl oz/1½ cups) home-made or low-salt
    chicken stock
80 ml (2½ fl oz/⅓ cup) manzanilla sherry
2 teaspoons finely shredded lemon zest
1 cinnamon stick
2 fresh bay leaves

herb and onion salad
½ red onion, very thinly sliced
1½ teaspoons finely grated lemon zest
1½ tablespoons small oregano leaves
1 handful very small mint leaves
¼ teaspoon ground cinnamon
2 teaspoons lemon juice

Serves 6

Preheat the oven to 160°C (315°F/Gas 2–3). Heat 2 tablespoons of the oil in a large heavy-based saucepan over medium heat. Add the onion and cook for 20 minutes, or until lightly golden, stirring now and then and making sure the onion doesn't burn. Add the garlic and cook for 2 minutes, then scatter the mixture over the base of a non-metallic baking dish just large enough to hold all the lamb chops in a single layer.

Add the remaining oil to the saucepan and increase the heat to high. Season the lamb lightly, then brown the chops well on each side, working in several batches. Arrange them over the onion in a single layer. Break the sprigs of rosemary, oregano, thyme and mint into smaller lengths and scatter over the lamb. Whisk together the yoghurt, stock, sherry and lemon zest until smooth, then pour over the lamb. Add the cinnamon stick and bay leaves.

Cover the dish tightly with foil and bake for 2½ hours. Remove the foil and cook for a further 1 hour, turning halfway through, or until the lamb is very tender and almost falling off the bone. The yoghurt will separate during cooking and look quite curdled.

Carefully lift the chops out into a serving dish and cover to keep warm. Discard the herb sprigs, bay leaves and cinnamon stick. Pour the sauce, including the onion, into a large saucepan and bring to the boil. Cook for about 15 minutes, or until thickened — the sauce will still look quite curdled but tastes delicious. If it looks too oily, skim off the excess oil.

In a small bowl, mix together all the the herb and onion salad ingredients. Spoon the sauce over the lamb, then spoon the salad over the top.

This recipe evokes happy memories of those sunny, colourful, Mediterranean stretches of Spain — coastal pockets lined with orange trees and olive groves — where you can pass the time sipping golden sherry and welcoming the warmth of the sun.

chicken with sherry, orange and olives

1 tablespoon olive oil
6 large chicken leg quarters (about 225 g/8 oz each)
20 g (3/4 oz) butter
1 large brown onion, finely chopped
1 carrot, finely chopped
1 celery stalk, finely chopped
1 fresh bay leaf
60 ml (2 fl oz/1/4 cup) fino (dry) sherry
60 ml (2 fl oz/1/4 cup) manzanilla sherry
2 1/2 teaspoons shredded orange zest
185 ml (6 fl oz/3/4 cup) strained, freshly squeezed
    orange juice
250 ml (9 fl oz/1 cup) home-made or low-salt
    chicken stock
150 g (5 1/2 oz/about 1 cup) Spanish anchovy-stuffed
    green olives
1 navel orange, peeled and cut into 1.5 cm
    (5/8 inch) cubes
1 handful flat-leaf (Italian) parsley

Serves 4–6

Preheat the oven to 180°C (350°F/Gas 4). Heat the oil in a large heavy-based frying pan over medium–high heat. Working in two or three batches, brown the chicken pieces for about 5 minutes each time, or until well browned. Sit them in a large roasting tin and set aside.

Pour off all but 1 tablespoon of oil from the pan and reduce the heat to medium. Add the butter and onion and cook for 8 minutes, or until the onion is lightly golden. Add the carrot, celery and bay leaf and cook for 10 minutes, or until the vegetables are softened and lightly golden.

Pour in all the sherry and cook for 1 minute, then add the orange zest, orange juice and stock. Bring to the boil, stirring well to scrape up any cooked-on bits. Pour the mixture over the chicken and bake for 1–1 1/4 hours, or until the chicken is golden and almost cooked through.

Pour the roasting juices into a small saucepan, then cover the chicken to keep it warm. Skim off any oil that settles on top of the sauce, then bring to the boil and allow to boil for 20 minutes, or until reduced and thickened slightly. Pour the sauce back over the chicken, scatter with the olives and orange and bake for a further 10 minutes. Serve scattered with the parsley, perhaps with creamy mashed potatoes or crispy potatoes and a green salad.

This special dinner soup is swimming with seafood and garnished with tasty *migas*, a wonderful Spanish version of croutons. *Migas* — bread fried with jamón, garlic and spring onions — are good enough to eat on their own, as they often are!

hearty seafood soup with migas

migas

6 slices bread, crusts removed, cut into 1.5 cm
($^{5}/_{8}$ inch) cubes
$^{1}/_{4}$ teaspoon salt dissolved in 60 ml (2 fl oz/$^{1}/_{4}$ cup) water
60 ml (2 fl oz/$^{1}/_{4}$ cup) olive oil
3 garlic cloves, chopped
2 slices jamón, prosciutto or jambon, chopped
$^{1}/_{2}$ teaspoon sweet paprika
2 spring onions (scallions), green part only, finely sliced

soup

250 g (9 oz) baby clams (vongole)
2 tablespoons olive oil
1 large red onion, finely chopped
1 large carrot, finely chopped
1 celery stalk, finely chopped
5 garlic cloves, crushed
1$^{1}/_{2}$ teaspoons smoked hot paprika, or 1 teaspoon
    sweet paprika and $^{1}/_{2}$ teaspoon cayenne pepper
3 slices jamón, prosciutto or jambon, finely chopped
1 fresh bay leaf
2 teaspoons finely chopped thyme
1 teaspoon ground fennel seeds
125 ml (4 fl oz/$^{1}/_{2}$ cup) fino (dry) sherry
2 long strips of orange zest, tied in a muslin
    (cheesecloth) bag
pinch of saffron threads
800 g (1 lb 12 oz) tomato passata (puréed tomatoes)
750 ml (26 fl oz/3 cups) home-made or low-salt fish stock
18 mussels, scrubbed and bearded
18 raw king prawns (shrimp), tails intact
6 cleaned baby squid, cut into 1 cm ($^{1}/_{2}$ inch) slices
400 g (14 oz) fish fillets, such as hake, snapper, red mullet
    (or any combination), cut into 3 cm (1$^{1}/_{4}$ inch) pieces

Serves 6

Start preparing the *migas* the night before. Put the bread cubes in a shallow dish, sprinkle with the salted water, mix well, then cover with plastic wrap and refrigerate overnight.

Soak the clams in several changes of fresh water for 2 hours.

While the clams are soaking, continue preparing the *migas*. Heat the oil in a non-stick frying pan over medium–low heat. Add the garlic and fry for 2–3 minutes, or until golden, then remove and discard the garlic. Reduce the heat to very low, add the bread and cook, stirring occasionally, for 40 minutes, or until crisp and golden. Add the jamón and paprika and cook for a further 3 minutes. Stir in the spring onion.

While the *migas* is cooking, make the soup. Heat the oil in a large stockpot over medium–high heat. Add the onion, carrot and celery and cook for 7 minutes, or until lightly golden. Stir in the garlic, paprika, jamón, bay leaf, thyme and ground fennel, then cook for 1 minute, or until fragrant. Add the sherry and bring to the boil, then add the orange zest bag, saffron, tomato passata, stock and 500 ml (17 fl oz/2 cups) of water. Bring to the boil again, then reduce the heat and simmer for 30 minutes.

Increase the heat to high and bring to the boil. Add the mussels and clams and cook for about 5 minutes, removing them as they open and setting them aside — discard any that remain closed after that time.

Add the prawns to the soup and cook for 1 minute, or until just starting to curl, then add the squid and cook for 1 minute. Scoop out the prawns and squid and set aside with the mussels. Cook the fish in the soup for 1 minute, then return all the seafood to the soup and cook for 2 minutes to heat through.

Discard the muslin bag and bay leaf, season the soup to taste, then evenly divide the seafood and broth among six wide, deep bowls. Serve the *migas* in a separate bowl for guests to spoon over the soup. If you're feeling really decadent, serve a little allioli on the side (see Basics, page 187).

Perfectly pink, succulent veal lightly perfumed with sherry is teamed with a creamy, crunchy-topped gratin and drizzled with a rich veal and sherry glaze. This recipe uses a 'nut' of veal, a boneless piece cut from the leg, tied with string to keep its shape.

sherry-poached veal with potato and anchovy gratin

potato and anchovy gratin

310 ml (10³/₄ fl oz/1¹/₄ cups) cream (whipping)

4 garlic cloves, crushed

3 tablespoons chopped parsley

1 teaspoon finely chopped thyme

3 teaspoons very finely chopped anchovies

pinch of freshly ground white pepper

700 g (1 lb 9 oz) desiree or other all-purpose potatoes, peeled, then very thinly sliced (use a mandolin if possible)

100 g (3¹/₂ oz/1¹/₄ cups) grated Manchego cheese

750 ml (26 fl oz/3 cups) home-made or low-salt chicken stock

375 ml (13 fl oz/1¹/₂ cups) fino (dry) sherry

125 ml (4 fl oz/¹/₂ cup) oloroso sherry

2 tablespoons sherry vinegar

2 fresh bay leaves

1 teaspoon whole black peppercorns

1 thyme sprig

1.25 kg (2 lb 12 oz) veal nut, tied with string

125 g (4¹/₂ oz/¹/₂ cup) veal glace (see Note)

Serves 4–6

Preheat the oven to 180°C (350°F/Gas 4). To make the potato and anchovy gratin, mix the cream, garlic, parsley, thyme, anchovies and white pepper in a large bowl with ¹/₂ teaspoon of salt. Add the potato slices and toss to coat well. Tip them into an 18 cm (7 inch) square cake tin or baking tin, gently spread them out and smooth the top. Cover tightly with foil and bake for 40 minutes, or until the potato is tender. Remove the foil, sprinkle with the cheese and cook for a further 20 minutes, or until the top is crisp and golden. Remove from the oven and rest for 10 minutes.

Meanwhile, put the stock, all the sherry, the vinegar, bay leaves, peppercorns and thyme sprig in a large saucepan with 1 litre (35 fl oz/4 cups) of cold water and bring to the boil over high heat. Allow to boil for 5 minutes, then add the veal. Return to the boil, then reduce the heat, cover and simmer for 20 minutes, turning regularly. Turn off the heat and allow the veal to sit in the hot stock for 30 minutes, then lift it out of the stock and cover to keep warm.

Pour 250 ml (9 fl oz/1 cup) of the poaching liquid into a small saucepan, stir in the veal glace and boil for 15 minutes, or until slightly syrupy.

Cut the potato gratin into equal portions and lift out onto serving plates. Trim the ends of the veal to neaten it, then cut it into thick slices. Arrange the veal over the potato and drizzle the poaching syrup over the top. This dish is superb with fresh greens, especially quickly wilted spinach.

Note: Veal glace is a thick, firm, jelly-like meat glaze (*glace de viande*), sold in jars at speciality stores and good delicatessens. It is made by boiling meat juices until they are reduced to a thick syrup.

Baking a fish in salt produces incredibly succulent flesh. Here it is gently permeated with herb and lemon flavours and dressed with a warm, infused olive oil — although a squeeze of lemon and a drizzle of extra virgin olive oil will suffice, at a pinch.

salt-baked fish with warm garlic and chilli oil

olive oil, for brushing
3–3.5 kg (6 lb 12 oz–7 lb 14 oz) whole snapper,
    cleaned and scaled
1 lemon, sliced
2–3 large flat-leaf (Italian) parsley sprigs
2–3 small thyme sprigs
4 spring onions (scallions), trimmed
3 fresh bay leaves
3 kg (6 lb 12 oz) rock salt
4 egg whites
lemon wedges (optional), to serve

warm garlic and chilli oil
125 ml (4 fl oz/1/2 cup) extra virgin olive oil
5 garlic cloves, very finely sliced
2 small red chillies, seeded and finely sliced

Serves 6–8

Preheat the oven to 180°C (350°F/Gas 4). Lightly oil a roasting tin large enough to hold the fish — if the fish is a little too big, remove the head. Fill the fish cavity with the lemon slices, parsley and thyme sprigs, spring onions and bay leaves. Brush the fish all over with a little oil.

Combine the salt and egg whites, then spread one-third of the mixture around the base of the roasting tin. Sit the fish on top, then cover it all over with the remaining salt mixture, packing the salt down to ensure the fish is thickly covered. Bake for 45 minutes — the salt crust will be firm and pale golden. Remove from the oven and rest for 15 minutes.

Meanwhile, make the warm garlic and chilli oil. Put the oil, garlic and chilli in a small saucepan over low heat and cook, stirring occasionally, for 10 minutes, or until the garlic is golden and aromatic. Set aside for the flavours to infuse, and reheat gently just before serving.

Crack the salt crust covering the fish, then remove the top layer of salt and skin. Remove the flesh using a fish slice or a large spoon and fork — it will come away from the bones very easily. Then, starting at the tail end, pull the bones off in one movement. Remove the bottom layer of flesh. Serve at once with lemon wedges, if desired, and with the warm garlic and chilli oil on the side for drizzling over. Wonderful with a simple, crisp salad.

Slowly cooked rabbit is tender and rich. In this hearty dish it is perfectly matched to a deep, smoky sauce, balanced by earthy lentils, silky, mellow eggplant and a subtle splash of sherry vinegar.

rabbit, eggplant and lentil stew

2 x 1.5 kg (3 lb 5 oz) young, farmed rabbits
60 ml (2 fl oz/1/4 cup) olive oil
2 red onions, cut into wedges
1 celery stalk, finely chopped
1 fresh bay leaf
4 garlic cloves, crushed
1 teaspoon smoked sweet paprika
1 tablespoon finely chopped oregano
1 small red chilli, seeded and finely chopped
800 g (1 lb 12 oz/3 1/4 cups) tinned chopped tomatoes
250 ml (9 fl oz/1 cup) fino (dry) sherry
60 ml (2 fl oz/1/4 cup) sherry vinegar
1.5 litres (52 fl oz/6 cups) home-made or low-salt chicken stock
1 large eggplant (aubergine), cut into 4 cm (1 1/2 inch) chunks
170 g (6 oz/3/4 cup) puy lentils or tiny blue-green lentils
oregano leaves, to garnish
80 g (2 3/4 oz/1/2 cup) roasted black olives (see page 27)

Serves 6–8

Cut each rabbit down the back into two halves. Carefully remove the saddle or fillet pieces that run down either side of the back, then cut each piece in half. Cut through where each front leg meets the body and set aside the legs. Next, cut through where each hind leg meets the body, then cut each hind leg at the joint to give four back leg pieces in total.

Heat the oil in a large, flameproof, heavy-based casserole dish over medium–high heat. Lightly season the rabbit pieces and brown well in two batches, for about 3 minutes on each side. Set aside.

Add the onion to the dish and cook for 3 minutes, or until lightly golden. Add the celery, bay leaf, garlic, paprika, oregano and chilli and cook for 2 minutes, or until fragrant. Add the tomato, sherry, sherry vinegar and stock and stir well, scraping up any cooked-on bits. Increase the heat to high, add the rabbit pieces and stir well. Bring to the boil, then reduce the heat, cover and simmer for 45 minutes.

Add the eggplant and lentils to the dish and stir well. Cook, uncovered, for a further 35–45 minutes, or until the rabbit is very tender and the lentils are tender but not mushy.

Remove the solids from the sauce and cover to keep warm. Boil the sauce for 25 minutes, or until thickened, then stir the solids back in and allow to heat through for a few minutes. Season to taste, then garnish with oregano leaves and roasted black olives. Serve with baby potatoes roasted in their skins with salt, oil and oregano.

Aromatic spices and sweet honey once again point to the Middle Eastern influence on Spanish cuisine. A wonderful main course, this recipe also makes a great summer buffet dish — just barbecue the lamb and serve on a large platter lined with the spinach salad.

spice-dusted lamb cutlets with honey

40 g (1½ oz/¼ cup) plucked dried muscatels
2 tablespoons Málaga wine, or a rich, sweet sherry
    such as Pedro Ximénez
80 g (2½ fl oz/¼ cup) honey
½ teaspoon grated lemon zest
16 lamb (frenched rib chop) cutlets
1½ tablespoons olive oil
1½ tablespoons pine nuts, toasted

spice mix

3 teaspoons ground cumin
2 teaspoons ground cinnamon
½ teaspoon smoked sweet paprika
½ teaspoon ground fennel seeds
1½ teaspoons salt

spinach salad

1 small red onion, very finely sliced
1 tablespoon lemon juice
2 tablespoons extra virgin olive oil
165 g (5¾ oz/3½ cups) baby English spinach leaves
1 handful flat-leaf (Italian) parsley

Serves 4–6

Steep the muscatels in the wine for 30 minutes to soften. Put them in a small saucepan with the honey, lemon zest and 60 ml (2 fl oz/¼ cup) of water. Bring to the boil for 2 minutes, then reduce the heat to a very low simmer and gently cook for 5 minutes. Turn off the heat and cover to keep warm.

Mix all the spice mix ingredients together on a plate, then press the cutlets into the spice mixture, turning to coat both sides. Set aside.

Start preparing the spinach salad. Put the onion, lemon juice and extra virgin olive oil in a large bowl with a pinch of salt. Mix together and set aside.

Heat the oil in a large frying pan over medium–high heat. Cook the lamb in three batches for about 2 minutes on each side, depending on the thickness of the cutlets and how well you like your lamb done. Set aside and cover lightly to keep warm.

Toss the spinach and parsley through the onion mixture, then divide the salad among serving plates and top each plate with the cutlets. Add the pine nuts to the honey sauce, drizzle over the lamb and serve immediately.

This flavoursome dish is in essence a kind of paella made using *fideos* — a Catalan noodle — instead of rice. Traditionally it is often laden with mixed cured and fresh meats, but I prefer the lighter seafood version.

seafood fideua

60 ml (2 fl oz/^{1}/$_4$ cup) olive oil
2 chorizo sausages, finely diced
18 raw king prawns (shrimp), peeled and deveined, tails intact
18 large scallops, without roe, and with any vein, membrane or hard white muscle removed
6 cleaned baby squid, sliced into 1 cm (^{1}/$_2$ inch) rings
1 large red onion, finely chopped
^{1}/$_2$ fennel bulb, diced
4 garlic cloves, chopped
1 bay leaf
1 small red chilli, seeded and finely chopped
2 teaspoons paprika
1 small red capsicum (pepper), cut into short thin strips
400 g (14 oz/1^1/$_2$ cups) tin chopped tomatoes
125 ml (4 fl oz/^{1}/$_2$ cup) fino (dry) sherry
pinch of saffron threads
large pinch of sugar
1.5 litres (52 fl oz/6 cups) home-made or low-salt chicken stock
400 g (14 oz) *fideos* noodles or spaghettini, broken into 3 cm (1^1/$_4$ inch) lengths
lemon wedges, to serve

picada
1 slice white bread, fried in olive oil until golden
1^1/$_2$ tablespoons pine nuts, toasted
1 large handful flat-leaf (Italian) parsley
3 garlic cloves, chopped
1^1/$_2$ teaspoons grated lemon zest
10 g (^{1}/$_4$ oz/^{1}/$_2$ cup loosely packed) fennel fronds

Serves 6–8

Heat 1 tablespoon of the oil in a very large, deep, heavy-based frying pan or paella pan over medium–high heat. Add the chorizo and cook for 5 minutes, or until slightly crispy. Add the prawns and cook for 1^1/$_2$ minutes, or until they just turn pink. Remove the prawns and chorizo with a slotted spoon and set aside.

Add a little more oil to the pan and sear the scallops in several batches for 30 seconds on each side, then set aside with the prawns. Cook the squid in the same pan for 1 minute, or until just starting to change colour, then add to the other seafood, cover and set aside.

Add the remaining oil, onion and fennel to the pan and cook for 10 minutes, or until softened and golden. Add the garlic, bay leaf, chilli, paprika and capsicum and cook for 2 minutes, or until softened. Add the tomato, sherry, saffron and sugar, bring to the boil and allow to boil for 10 minutes, stirring often, until the sauce is thick and pulpy.

Meanwhile, pour the stock into a large saucepan. Bring to the boil over high heat, then reduce the heat to a slow simmer.

Add the noodles to the tomato sauce and stir to coat. Pour in the simmering stock, stir to thoroughly combine, then cook, stirring only once or twice, for about 20 minutes, or until almost all the liquid is absorbed. Stir in all the seafood and chorizo and cook for another few minutes, or until the seafood is heated through and the noodles are tender.

While the noodles are cooking, put all the picada ingredients in a food processor and blend to a paste. Stir the picada through the noodles just before serving, or serve in a separate bowl for guests to stir through themselves. Serve the noodles with lemon wedges.

Sweet and spicy red capsicum jam, flavoured with tomato, chilli and paprika, is a superb accompaniment to these savoury chicken breasts. Any leftover jam will keep well and makes a delicious sandwich relish.

crisp cumin chicken with red capsicum jam

red capsicum jam
2 tablespoons olive oil
1 red onion, finely chopped
1 large red capsicum (pepper), finely diced
2 garlic cloves, finely chopped
1 small red chilli, seeded and finely chopped
large pinch of smoked sweet paprika
125 g (4 oz/½ cup) tomato passata (puréed tomatoes)
1½ tablespoons sherry vinegar
2 tablespoons soft brown sugar

2 teaspoons ground cumin
1½ teaspoons salt
4 boneless chicken breasts, skin on
1 tablespoon olive oil

Serves 4

To make the red capsicum jam, heat the oil in a saucepan over medium–low heat, add the onion and cook for 15–20 minutes, stirring occasionally, or until lightly golden. Add the capsicum, garlic, chilli and paprika and cook for 10 minutes, or until the capsicum has softened. Add the tomato passata, sherry vinegar, sugar and 125 ml (4 fl oz/½ cup) of water and bring to the boil. Reduce to a low simmer and cook for 2 hours, stirring regularly, until the jam is thick and pulpy and has darkened slightly. Season to taste.

Meanwhile, combine the cumin and salt, then rub it all over the chicken breasts. Refrigerate, uncovered, until ready to cook.

Heat the oil in a large frying pan over medium–high heat. Add the chicken breasts, skin side down, and cook for 3 minutes, or until the skin is golden and crispy. Turn and cook for a further 5 minutes, or until just cooked through.

Serve the chicken with the jam, perhaps on slices of grilled eggplant (aubergine), or large saffron rice cakes (see page 79) with a green salad on the side.

A modern twist on the much-loved Basque dish of stuffed spider crab baked in the shell (*txangurro*). Fresh crab meat is best, but you can also use tinned crab meat (squeeze out all the excess moisture first), or finely chopped cooked prawns (shrimp).

txangurro ravioli

crab filling

10 g (1/4 oz) butter

1 tablespoon olive oil

1/2 leek, white part only, finely chopped

1 small carrot, very finely diced

1 fresh bay leaf

2 garlic cloves, crushed

1 1/2 teaspoons chopped thyme

1 tablespoon brandy

2 tablespoons white wine

250 g (9 oz/1 cup) chopped tinned tomatoes

pinch of caster (superfine) sugar

170 ml (5 1/2 fl oz/2/3 cup) home-made or low-salt
   fish or chicken stock

200 g (7 oz/1 1/4 cups) cooked crab meat, picked over

1 tablespoon chopped flat-leaf (Italian) parsley

8 fresh lasagne sheets, each measuring about
   17 x 28 cm (6 1/2 x 11 1/4 inches)

1 egg, lightly beaten

300 ml (10 1/2 fl oz) cream (whipping)

1 fresh bay leaf, extra

60 g (2 1/4 oz/2/3 cup) grated Manchego cheese

topping

2 tablespoons olive oil

3 slices white bread, crusts removed, cut into 3 mm
   (1/8 inch) cubes

1 tablespoon chopped flat-leaf (Italian) parsley

smoked sweet paprika, for sprinkling

Serves 4 as a main, 8 as a starter

Start by making the crab filling. Heat the butter and oil in a saucepan over medium heat. Add the leek, carrot and bay leaf and cook for 10 minutes, or until lightly golden. Add the garlic and thyme and cook for 30 seconds, or until fragrant. Carefully add the brandy and wine and bring to the boil. Add the tomato, sugar and stock, bring to the boil, then reduce the heat and simmer rapidly for 30–35 minutes, or until the mixture is thick and pulpy and the liquid has evaporated. Remove from the heat and stir in the crab meat and parsley. Season to taste, allow to cool slightly, then refrigerate until cold.

Lay a lasagne sheet horizontally on your workbench. Imagine a vertical line dividing the sheet into two large squares, then place a neat mound (about 2 tablespoons) of the crab filling in the centre of each square. Brush a little beaten egg around the edges of the pasta, avoiding the crab mixture.

Lay a second lasagne sheet over the top, then cut down the imaginary line to separate the two large squares. Press down the edges to seal, then trim 1 cm (1/2 inch) off each outside edge using a large, sharp knife, to make a neater edge and help seal the lasagne sheets. Firmly seal the edges together, crimping them with a fork if necessary, so the filling doesn't leak out during cooking. Repeat with the remaining six sheets of lasagne to make a total of eight large ravioli. Refrigerate for 30 minutes, or until ready to cook.

Meanwhile, start making the topping. Heat the oil in a small frying pan over medium–high heat, add the bread cubes and sauté for 2 minutes, or until golden and crisp. Drain on crumpled paper towels.

Bring a large saucepan of salted water to the boil. Meanwhile, put the cream and remaining bay leaf in a small saucepan over high heat and bring to the boil. Remove from the heat, discard the bay leaf, add the cheese and stir until it melts and forms a smooth sauce. Set aside.

In two batches, add the ravioli to the boiling water. When the water returns to the boil, cook for 1 minute, or until the pasta is *al dente* and the filling is hot. Drain well, then divide among serving plates. Spoon over some sauce, scatter with the bread cubes, sprinkle with a little parsley and paprika and serve.

Roasted pork is complemented by a compôte of fennel, apples and muscatels and sauced with a lovely fennel jus, both natural accompaniments for the rich, tender pork meat, covered in the crispiest of crackling.

roast pork belly with fennel

fennel jus

3 tablespoons olive oil
2 kg (4 lb 8 oz) pork bones
1 large brown onion, chopped
1 large carrot, chopped
2 celery stalks, chopped
1 1/2 tablespoons fennel seeds
1 fresh bay leaf
1 tablespoon fennel fronds
2 garlic cloves, roughly chopped
dash of dry anis (optional), or other dry aniseed liqueur

1.5 kg (3 lb 5 oz) piece of boneless pork belly
1 1/2 tablespoons sea salt flakes

fennel and apple compôte

40 g (1 1/2 oz/1/4 cup) plucked dried muscatels,
    or other raisins
60 ml (2 fl oz/1/4 cup) manzanilla sherry
20 g (3/4 oz) butter
12 small French shallots (eschalots)
1 small fennel bulb, cut into 1.5 cm (5/8 inch) cubes
2 apples, cored, peeled and cut into 1.5 cm (5/8 inch)
    cubes
1 teaspoon lemon juice
1 teaspoon sugar

Serves 6

To make the fennel jus, heat 1 tablespoon of the oil in a large saucepan over medium–high heat. Add a third of the pork bones and brown well on all sides for about 8 minutes, then remove. Working in another two batches, brown the remaining pork bones in the remaining oil and remove. Add the onion to the same pan and cook, stirring occasionally, for 6 minutes, or until lightly golden. Add the carrot, celery, fennel seeds and bay leaf and cook for another 10 minutes, or until softened and lightly golden. Add the fennel fronds, garlic and 4 litres (140 fl oz) of cold water, bring to the boil, then reduce the heat and simmer for 4 hours. Strain into a clean pan, then bring to the boil, remove any scum that forms, and cook for a further 1 hour, or until slightly syrupy. Stir in a few drops of anis if desired.

About halfway through cooking, preheat the oven to 200°C (400°F/Gas 6). Sit the pork on a rack in a roasting tin and rub all over with the sea salt flakes. Roast for 1 1/2 hours, or until the crackling is very crisp and the pork is cooked through. Remove from the heat, lightly cover and rest for 10 minutes.

While the pork is roasting, make the fennel and apple compôte. Put the muscatels and sherry in a small saucepan, bring to the boil then set aside to soak for 15 minutes. In another saucepan, melt the butter over medium–high heat, add the shallots and cook for 5 minutes, or until lightly golden, shaking the pan occasionally. Add the fennel and apple and cook, stirring regularly, for 15 minutes, or until lightly golden. Stir in the muscatels and sherry, lemon juice and sugar and cook for 15 minutes, stirring occasionally, or until the apple is soft but not mushy and the compôte has a golden-hued glaze. Set aside.

Cut the rested pork into six equal portions and serve with the gently reheated compôte and jus. Delicious with lightly cooked young vegetables.

Pan-fried salmon finds a spritely accompaniment in a lemony herb and egg salsa, a welcome change from the rich sauces traditionally served with salmon. This unusual pairing is perfect for the warmer months. Any leftover salsa can be tossed through pasta.

salmon with herb and egg salsa

herb and egg salsa
2 hard-boiled eggs
1 tablespoon pine nuts, toasted
10 almonds, toasted
5 walnuts, toasted
1 large handful flat-leaf (Italian) parsley
2^1/$_2$ tablespoons oregano leaves
25–30 g (1 oz/1 bunch) chives
1 teaspoon finely grated lemon zest
3 garlic cloves, crushed
80 ml (2^1/$_2$ fl oz/^{1}/$_3$ cup) extra virgin olive oil
2 tablespoons lemon juice

4 x 200 g (7 oz) salmon fillets
olive oil, for pan-frying

Serves 4

To make the herb and egg salsa, finely chop the eggs, all the nuts and all the herbs and put them in a bowl with the lemon zest, garlic, oil and lemon juice. Mix to form a loose paste, then season well and set aside.

Season the salmon with salt and black pepper. Heat a little oil in a large heavy-based frying pan over high heat. Add the fish, skin side down, and cook for 4–5 minutes, or until the skin is crispy. Turn and cook for another 2–3 minutes for a rare to medium result, or a little longer if you like your salmon cooked through — the exact cooking time will depend on the thickness of the fillets and how rare you like your salmon.

Serve the salmon, skin side up, over some lightly cooked asparagus or beans and dollop the salsa over the top. Serve any extra salsa in a bowl for guests to help themselves.

Spanish quince paste (*membrillo*), melted together with raisiny Málaga wine and fresh orange juice, makes an intense fruity glaze for rich duck and marries well with earthy lentils and crunchy nuts.

duck breast with lentils and quince sauce

4 x 200 g (7 oz) duck breasts, rinsed and patted dry
265 g (9^1/$_2$ oz/1^1/$_4$ cups) puy lentils or tiny
    blue-green lentils
1 tablespoon olive oil
6 blanched almonds
6 skinned hazelnuts
20 g (^{3}/$_4$ oz) butter
1 small red onion, finely diced
1 small carrot, finely diced
1 celery stalk, finely diced
125 ml (4 fl oz/^{1}/$_2$ cup) home-made or low-salt
    chicken stock
2 teaspoons finely chopped sage
1 large handful flat-leaf (Italian) parsley, finely chopped
1 teaspoon very finely chopped thyme
2 teaspoons oil, extra
sage leaves, extra, to garnish

quince sauce
50 g (1^3/$_4$ oz/1^1/$_2$ tablespoons) quince paste
2 tablespoons Málaga wine, or a rich, sweet sherry
    such as Pedro Ximénez
60 ml (2 fl oz/^{1}/$_4$ cup) strained, freshly squeezed
    orange juice
60 ml (2 fl oz/^{1}/$_4$ cup) home-made or low-salt
    chicken stock

Serves 4

Season the duck breasts all over with salt, then place on a tray, skin side up, and sprinkle with a little more salt. Refrigerate, uncovered, until ready to cook.

Put the lentils in a saucepan with 1.5 litres (52 fl oz/6 cups) of cold water. Bring to the boil, then reduce the heat and simmer for 20–30 minutes, or until tender — the actual cooking time will depend on the age of the lentils. Drain well and set aside.

Mix all the quince sauce ingredients together in a saucepan. Bring to the boil, mashing any lumps of quince paste until smooth, and cook over medium–high heat for 3 minutes, or until slightly syrupy. Remove from the heat. If your quince sauce seems a bit fibrous, you might like to strain it through a sieve.

Heat the olive oil in a saucepan over medium–high heat and add the almonds and hazelnuts. Cook, stirring, for 1^1/$_2$ minutes, or until golden. Drain on crumpled paper towels and allow to cool slightly.

Melt the butter in the same pan. Add the onion, carrot and celery and cook, stirring occasionally, for 10 minutes, or until lightly golden. Add the stock and cook, stirring occasionally, until the liquid is almost absorbed. Finely chop the nuts and mix them through with the lentils, sage, parsley and thyme. Season to taste, remove from the heat and cover to keep warm.

Heat the extra oil in a large heavy-based frying pan over medium heat. Cook the duck, skin side down, for about 5 minutes to render the fat, then remove the duck from the pan. Pour off the fat and put the pan back over high heat. Add the duck, skin side up, and cook for 4–5 minutes to seal, then turn and cook for another 2 minutes, or until the skin is crisp and golden. Remove from the heat, cover lightly and rest for 5 minutes.

Gently reheat the lentils and quince sauce. Divide the lentils among four plates in neat mounds and top with a sliced duck breast. Drizzle with the quince sauce, garnish with a few sage leaves and serve immediately.

Baked cannelloni is popular in Spain's Catalan region, but differs from the Italian original. This flavoursome version is filled with chorizo, morcilla and jamón, all cooked in a sherry-spiked tomato sauce, under a creamy Manchego cheese topping.

catalan cannelloni

filling

3 teaspoons olive oil
1 small red onion, finely chopped
1 carrot, finely chopped
1 celery stalk, finely chopped
1 chorizo sausage, finely diced
2 garlic cloves, crushed
small pinch of ground cloves
500 g (1 lb 2 oz) white butifarra sausages, or other mild, fresh pork sausages
1 morcilla sausage
2 slices jamón, prosciutto or jambon, very finely chopped
120 g (4^1/$_4$ oz/1^1/$_2$ cups) fresh, soft white breadcrumbs
80 ml (2^1/$_2$ fl oz/^{1}/$_3$ cup) cream (whipping)
freshly ground white pepper, to taste

tomato sauce

1^1/$_2$ tablespoons olive oil
1 large red onion, finely chopped
2 garlic cloves, crushed
3 x 400 g (14 oz) tins chopped tomatoes
125 ml (4 fl oz/^{1}/$_2$ cup) fino (dry) sherry
1^1/$_2$ teaspoons finely chopped thyme
^{1}/$_2$ teaspoon caster (superfine) sugar

white sauce

30 g (1 oz) butter
30 g (1 oz/^{1}/$_4$ cup) plain (all-purpose) flour
935 ml (33 fl oz/4 cups) milk
1 fresh bay leaf
2 tablespoons finely chopped parsley
80 g (2^3/$_4$ oz/^{3}/$_4$ cup) grated Manchego cheese

24 instant cannelloni tubes (250 g/9 oz in total), each about 10 cm (4 inches) long

Serves 8–10

First, make the filling. Heat the oil in a small frying pan over medium–high heat. Add the onion, carrot, celery and chorizo and cook, stirring occasionally, for 20 minutes, or until soft and lightly golden. Stir in the garlic and cloves and cook for 1 minute, then set aside to cool.

Peel the skin off the butifarra and the morcilla and discard. Finely chop the morcilla and put it in a bowl with the butifarra, jamón and breadcrumbs. Mash the mixture together, then mix well with your hands to form an even paste. Mix through the cream, then the cooled vegetable mixture, and season with a little white pepper. Cover and refrigerate until ready to use.

To make the tomato sauce, heat the oil in a small saucepan over medium–high heat. Add the onion and cook, stirring occasionally, for 5 minutes, or until lightly golden. Add the garlic, tomato, sherry, thyme, sugar and 125 ml (4 fl oz/^{1}/$_2$ cup) of water. Bring to the boil, then reduce the heat and simmer for 20 minutes, or until thickened slightly. Season lightly.

While the tomato sauce is simmering, make the white sauce. Melt the butter in a saucepan over medium heat, then add the flour and cook, stirring, for 2 minutes. Remove from the heat and gradually whisk in the milk. Add the bay leaf, then put the pan back over the heat and cook, stirring, for 12 minutes, or until thickened to a saucy consistency. Remove from the heat and allow to cool, then discard the bay leaf and stir in the parsley and cheese. Season to taste.

Preheat the oven to 180°C (350°F/Gas 4). Using a piping (icing) bag, push the meat filling into the cannelloni tubes. Pour some of the tomato sauce over the base of a 30 x 33 cm (12 x 13 inch) baking dish, then sit the filled tubes over the top in a single layer. Pour the remaining tomato sauce over the top and smooth the surface. Pour the white sauce evenly over the top, then cover with foil and bake for 30 minutes.

Remove the foil and cook for another 1 hour, or until the topping is golden and bubbling and the cannelloni filling is cooked all the way through. Serve at once, with a crisp green salad.

Mushrooms, truffle oil, olives and Manchego make a brilliant gourmet butter for a top-grade piece of fillet steak. Spread any leftover butter over some hot toast and top with a poached egg and sautéed field mushrooms for a spectacular breakfast dish.

fillet of beef with cep, olive and manchego butter

cep, olive and manchego butter

1 tablespoon dried cep (porcini) mushroom pieces
100 g (3^1/$_2$ oz) butter, softened
60 g (2^1/$_4$ oz/^{2}/$_3$ cup) finely grated Manchego cheese
1 scant teaspoon black truffle oil
4 small pitted black olives (preferably stored in olive oil),
   very finely chopped
1 small garlic clove, crushed

750 ml (26 fl oz/3 cups) home-made or low-salt beef
   or veal stock
1 garlic clove, bruised
2 teaspoons Pedro Ximénez or oloroso sherry
olive oil, for pan-frying
4 x 200 g (7 oz) beef fillets

Serves 4

Soak the mushroom pieces in 2 tablespoons of hot water for 15 minutes, or until soft. Drain, reserving the soaking liquid. Finely chop the mushrooms, put them in a bowl and set aside.

Put the reserved soaking liquid in a small saucepan with the stock and the bruised garlic clove. Bring to the boil for 10 minutes, then reduce the heat and simmer for 50 minutes, or until the liquid is reduced to about 60 ml (2 fl oz/ ^{1}/$_4$ cup). Strain through a very fine sieve and stir in the sherry. Set aside.

To make the cep, olive and Manchego butter, add the butter to the chopped mushrooms, along with the cheese, truffle oil, olives and garlic. Mix well, then season to taste with salt and a little freshly cracked black pepper. Spoon onto a sheet of plastic wrap, into a log 12 cm (4^1/$_2$ inches) long. Roll the plastic up, twisting the loose ends in opposite directions to form a log of butter about 2 cm (^{3}/$_4$ inch) thick. Refrigerate for 1 hour, or until firm. Take the butter out of the refrigerator just before you're ready to serve.

Heat a little oil in a large heavy-based frying pan over high heat. Season the steaks and cook for 4–5 minutes on each side for a medium–rare result, or until done to your liking. Remove from the pan, cover and rest for 5 minutes.

While the steaks are resting, gently reheat the sauce, and slice the chilled log of butter. Place the steaks on serving plates, top with sliced butter and drizzle with a little sauce. Wonderful with fresh steamed asparagus.

Atun blanco or bonito del norte — white tuna to us — is superior-quality meat from the albacore tuna. This superb fish is often packed in jars of olive oil from Spain or Italy. Mixed with golden garlic, chilli and lemon, this quick, easy dish is summer on a plate.

summer pasta with tuna

500 g (1 lb 2 oz) dried spaghettini or linguine
540 g (1 lb 3 oz) jars good-quality white tuna
   (atun blanco or bonito del norte) in olive oil,
   drained and oil reserved
6 garlic cloves, finely chopped
4 anchovies, very finely chopped
1/2 teaspoon smoked sweet paprika
1 small red chilli, seeded and finely chopped
2 large, very ripe tomatoes, chopped
1 large handful flat-leaf (Italian) parsley, chopped
1 tablespoon chopped oregano
1/4 teaspoon finely grated lemon zest
2 tablespoons lemon juice

Serves 4

Bring a large saucepan of salted water to the boil. Add the pasta and cook until al dente, following the packet instructions.

Meanwhile, strain the reserved oil from the tuna through a fine sieve. You should have about 170 ml (5 1/2 fl oz/2/3 cup) — if not, top it up with some extra virgin olive oil, and pour it into a small saucepan with the garlic, anchovies, paprika and chilli. Cook over medium–low heat for 4–5 minutes, stirring occasionally, until the garlic is golden.

Put the tuna in a large serving bowl and break it up into large chunks. Add the tomato, parsley, oregano, lemon zest and lemon juice and stir to combine.

Drain the pasta and add it to the tuna mixture. Pour the warm oil mixture over and toss well to combine. Season to taste with salt and freshly cracked black pepper and serve.

This fresh twist on the traditional Spanish dish of potatoes in allioli — normally served as a tapas offering — makes a great new-style potato salad that is perfect with seared veal cutlets. It is also wonderful with chicken or salmon.

veal cutlets with potatoes in hazelnut allioli

700 g (1 lb 9 oz) kipfler (fingerling) potatoes,
    washed but not peeled
4 veal (frenched rib chop) cutlets (about 225 g/
    8 oz each)
olive oil, for pan-frying
sage or celery leaves, to garnish
chopped toasted hazelnuts (optional), for sprinkling

hazelnut allioli
1/2 quantity of allioli (see Basics, page 187)
35 g (1 1/4 oz/1/4 cup) hazelnuts, toasted and finely
    chopped
2 spring onions (scallions), finely sliced
1 celery stalk, very finely diced
1 1/2 tablespoons finely chopped sage
1 large handful flat-leaf (Italian) parsley, chopped
1 1/2 tablespoons lemon juice
1 tablespoon sherry vinegar

Serves 4

Put the whole potatoes in a large saucepan and cover with cold water. Bring to the boil and allow to boil for 18 minutes, or until tender. Drain and allow to cool slightly, then peel and cut into 2 cm (3/4 inch) slices on the diagonal.

Put all the hazelnut allioli ingredients in a large bowl. Mix together well, then add the warm potatoes, toss gently and season to taste. Set aside.

Season the veal lightly with salt and freshly cracked black pepper. Heat a little oil in a large heavy-based frying pan or chargrill pan over high heat. Cook the cutlets for 3–4 minutes on each side, depending on their thickness — the veal should still be just a little pink in the middle. Remove from the heat, cover with foil and rest for a few minutes.

Serve the veal garnished with sage or celery leaves and chopped toasted hazelnuts if desired, with the potato salad on the side.

Samfaina is a Catalan sauce similar to French ratatouille. It is used as a base for many dishes — particularly seafood and poultry — but is also superb as a relish and can even be tossed through pasta. Here, an olive crust on the fish adds a savoury note.

swordfish samfaina

samfaina

80 ml (2^1/$_2$ fl oz/^{1}/$_3$ cup) olive oil

1 red onion, chopped

1 small eggplant (aubergine), cut into 1.5 cm (^{5}/$_8$ inch) cubes

1 large red capsicum (pepper), cut into 1.5 cm (^{5}/$_8$ inch) cubes

1 zucchini (courgette), cut into 1.5 cm (^{5}/$_8$ inch) cubes

3 garlic cloves, finely chopped

1 fresh bay leaf

60 ml (2 fl oz/^{1}/$_4$ cup) dry white wine

400 g (14 oz/1^2/$_3$ cups) tin chopped tomatoes

1 teaspoon caster (superfine) sugar

large pinch of sea salt

60 g (2^1/$_4$ oz/^{1}/$_2$ cup) pitted black olives

2 spring onions (scallions), chopped

1 handful flat-leaf (Italian) parsley

2 slices white bread, crusts removed, torn into smaller pieces

60 ml (2 fl oz/^{1}/$_4$ cup) olive oil

4 x 200 g (7 oz) swordfish steaks

olive oil, extra, for pan-frying

Serves 4

To make the *samfaina*, put the oil in a saucepan over medium heat, add the onion and cook for 15 minutes, or until golden, stirring occasionally. Add the eggplant, capsicum and zucchini and cook for 10 minutes, or until lightly golden, stirring occasionally. Add the garlic, bay leaf, wine, tomato, sugar and sea salt. Bring to the boil, reduce the heat and simmer, stirring occasionally, for 45 minutes, or until pulpy — you may need to add a little water to the pan to stop the sauce sticking.

Put the olives in a food processor with the spring onion, parsley, bread and oil and blend to a paste.

Preheat the grill (broiler) to high. Trim the swordfish of any sinew and dark spots, and season lightly. Heat a little oil in a large, heavy-based frying pan over high heat and sear the fish on one side for 1^1/$_2$ minutes, then turn and cook the other side for 45 seconds only. Remove from the heat and turn the fish out onto a foil-lined grill tray or baking tray, with the lesser cooked side facing upwards.

Neatly spread one-quarter of the olive mixture over each piece of fish, then grill (broil) for 1^1/$_2$ minutes, or until the fish is just cooked through and the olive topping is lightly crusted.

Divide the *samfaina* among four serving plates. Top each with a swordfish steak and serve immediately.

Beef cheeks become very tender and gelatinous on slow cooking, so they are perfect
fare for stews and casseroles. You might enjoy this beautiful rustic dish on a visit to a
sidreria (cider house) in the apple-growing districts of Spain.

beef cheeks in cider

1.5 kg (3 lb 5 oz) beef cheeks (see Note)
20 g (³/₄ oz) butter
2 tablespoons olive oil
1 large red onion, chopped
2 large carrots, cut into 2 cm (³/₄ inch) chunks
1 large celery stalk, diced
3 slices jamón, prosciutto or jambon, chopped
1 fresh bay leaf
2 garlic cloves, finely chopped
560 ml (19¹/₄ fl oz/2¹/₄ cups) home-made or
    low-salt beef stock
560 ml (19¹/₄ fl oz/2¹/₄ cups) Spanish *sidra*, or other
    alcoholic apple cider
1 tablespoon cider vinegar
2 large turnips or parsnips (about 400 g/14 oz in total),
    cut into thick batons
400 g (14 oz) tin chickpeas, well drained
1 tablespoon soft brown sugar

topping
1 green apple, cored but not peeled, finely diced
1 handful flat-leaf (Italian) parsley, chopped
25 g (1 oz/¹/₄ cup) walnuts, toasted and chopped

Serves 6

Trim the sinew and excess fat from the beef cheeks — this should leave just
over 1 kg (2 lb 4 oz) of meat. Cut each cheek in half. Heat the butter and oil in
a large flameproof casserole dish over medium heat. Add the onion and carrot
and cook for 20 minutes, or until dark golden, stirring occasionally. Remove
with a slotted spoon and set aside. Add the celery, jamón, bay leaf and garlic
and cook for 2 minutes, or until softened. Remove and add to the carrot.

Add a little more oil to the pan if needed and increase the heat to high. Quickly
season the beef cheeks, then brown them well in two batches, for 6 minutes
each time. Return all the beef to the pan with the vegetable mixture and stir
in the stock, cider and vinegar. Bring to the boil, then reduce the heat, cover
and simmer for 2 hours, skimming any scum off the surface during cooking.

Stir in the turnip, chickpeas and sugar and cook, uncovered, for 30 minutes,
or until the beef is very tender and the sauce has thickened slightly. Remove
the solids from the pan and cover to keep warm. Bring the sauce to the boil
and cook for 20 minutes, or until thickened slightly. Return the vegetables
and meat to the pan and stir to coat and gently heat through. Season to taste.

Mix the topping ingredients together and serve in a separate bowl for
sprinkling over the meat. Divide the beef cheeks among six serving plates
and serve with a creamy mash or polenta.

Note: Beef cheeks are a specialty cut that you will probably need to ask your
butcher to order in for you, although sometimes they may have them frozen.
They are in fact from the face of the cow, not the rump!

Ajo blanco is a white soup traditionally made from lots of garlic, olive oil and almonds (or bread). Here the flavours are blended with cauliflower for a lighter yet thicker version, which makes a beautiful base for juicy chargrilled tuna.

tuna steaks with cauliflower ajo blanco

cauliflower ajo blanco
500 g (1 lb 2 oz) cauliflower, broken into florets
1 thyme sprig
500 ml (17 fl oz/2 cups) home-made or low-salt
  chicken stock
125 ml (4 fl oz/1/2 cup) cream (whipping)
6 garlic cloves, crushed
50 g (1³/4 oz/1/2 cup) ground almonds
2 tablespoons olive oil

6 bulb spring onions (scallions), trimmed
20 g (³/4 oz) butter
2 tablespoons sherry vinegar, plus extra, for drizzling
1 teaspoon caster (superfine) sugar
4 x 200 g (7 oz) tuna steaks
olive oil, for brushing
60 g (2¹/4 oz/1/2 cup) roasted black olives (see page 27)
1 tablespoon extra virgin olive oil

Serves 4

To make the cauliflower *ajo blanco*, put the cauliflower in a saucepan with the thyme, stock, cream and half the garlic. Stir together, bring to the boil, then reduce the heat, cover and simmer for 8 minutes, or until the cauliflower is soft. Lift the cauliflower out with a slotted spoon and set aside. Increase the heat to high and boil the sauce for 20 minutes, or until reduced and thickened slightly.

Put the cauliflower in a food processor and blend until smooth. Stir into the simmering sauce with the ground almonds and cook for 3–4 minutes, or until thickened to a very thick soup or purée. Remove from the heat and stir in the oil and remaining garlic. Remove the thyme sprig, season to taste and set aside.

Trim the spring onions, leaving about 2 cm (³/4 inch) of green stem attached to each bulb. Cook in a small saucepan of boiling water for 4 minutes, or until just tender. Drain, reserving 2 tablespoons of the cooking water. When the spring onions have cooled slightly, cut them in half from top to bottom.

Melt the butter in a small frying pan over medium heat. Add the spring onions, cut side down, and cook for 2 minutes, or until golden underneath, then remove and set aside. Add the sherry vinegar, reserved cooking liquid and sugar to the pan and bring to the boil. Cook for 2 minutes, or until glazy, then put the onions back in and turn to coat.

Gently reheat the *ajo blanco*. Meanwhile, heat a large heavy-based chargrill pan to medium–high. Season the tuna steaks, then brush the pan with a little oil and cook the tuna for 1¹/2 minutes on each side for rare, or for about 2¹/2 minutes on each side for medium–rare.

Divide the *ajo blanco* neatly among four plates and top with the tuna. Arrange the glazed spring onions and olives over the top and serve drizzled with the extra virgin olive oil and a little extra sherry vinegar.

The cuisine of northern Spain is greatly influenced by neighbouring France. Here, tender slow-cooked duck legs are infused with Spanish spices and blasted in a hot oven to crisp the skin, teamed with a fresh, sweet, crisp and peppery salad.

crispy duck with fennel salad

4 duck leg quarters (about 220 g/7³/₄ oz each)
1¹/₂ tablespoons rock salt
3 garlic cloves, chopped
3 fresh bay leaves, torn
2¹/₂ tablespoons fennel seeds, toasted and lightly crushed
1 tablespoon cumin seeds, toasted and lightly crushed
1 tablespoon finely chopped thyme
3 x 350 g (12 oz) tins duck fat
4 garlic cloves, extra, finely chopped

fennel salad
4 baby fennel bulbs (about 200 g/7 oz each), with fronds
2 large handfuls flat-leaf (Italian) parsley
1 large celery stalk, finely sliced on the diagonal
1 large crisp apple, cored and very finely sliced
1/2 red onion, very finely sliced
2 tablespoons cider vinegar
1 tablespoon lemon juice
2 tablespoons extra virgin olive oil
1 teaspoon caster (superfine) sugar

Serves 4

Sit the duck legs in a large non-metallic baking dish. Combine the rock salt, garlic, bay leaves, fennel seeds, cumin and thyme in a small bowl, then rub the mixture all over the duck. Cover tightly with several layers of plastic wrap and refrigerate for 24 hours.

Rinse the duck and pat dry with paper towels. Melt the duck fat in a large, deep, heavy-based saucepan over low heat. Stir in the extra garlic, add the duck and cook for 2¹/₄ to 2¹/₂ hours, or until the meat is very tender but not falling from the bone. Remove the duck to a large non-metallic dish, then strain the fat over the top, making sure the duck is completely covered. Refrigerate until ready to use. The duck confit will last in this way for several weeks.

When you're ready to serve the duck, preheat the oven to 220°C (425°F/Gas 7). Lightly scrape the excess fat from the duck and wrap any exposed bones with foil so they don't burn. Put the duck on a baking tray and bake for 20–25 minutes, or until the skin is crispy and the meat is heated through.

Meanwhile, prepare the fennel salad. Chop the fennel fronds and very thinly slice the bulbs. Toss them in a large serving bowl with the parsley, celery, apple and onion. Whisk together the vinegar, lemon juice, oil and sugar, season to taste, then pour over the salad and toss well.

Serve the duck legs whole with the salad on the side, or pull the meat off the bones, then shred the meat and toss it through the salad.

Note: Duck fat is quite expensive. When you confit a duck in fat, the legs will release plenty of extra fat, which you can strain through a fine sieve and refrigerate for use in other recipes, such as the Spanish-style duck rillette recipe on page 75. Duck fat will keep in the refrigerator for up to 2 months.

This creamy dish of tender lamb and sweet spring vegetables is enriched by the addition of egg yolks and cream in the final stages of cooking. A splash of lemon juice and dry sherry give it a fresh, zesty lift.

lamb shanks with artichokes and lemon

2 tablespoons olive oil
6 large lamb shanks (about 250 g/9 oz each)
1 large leek, white part only, chopped
1 large carrot, chopped
1 celery stalk, chopped
1 fresh bay leaf
3 garlic cloves, crushed
250 ml (9 fl oz/1 cup) white wine
1 litre (35 fl oz/4 cups) home-made or low-salt chicken stock
2 teaspoons finely chopped oregano
2 teaspoons chopped thyme
2 large strips of lemon zest
175 g (6 oz/1 bunch) asparagus, cut into 3 cm (1¼ inch) lengths
70 g (2½ oz/½ cup) fresh baby peas
4 egg yolks
170 ml (5½ fl oz/⅔ cup) cream (whipping)
1 tablespoon lemon juice
2 teaspoons fino (dry) sherry
350 g (12 oz) jar artichoke hearts in olive oil, rinsed and drained well

Serves 6

Heat the oil in a large, heavy-based, flameproof casserole dish over medium–high heat. Lightly season the lamb shanks. Working in two batches, brown the shanks on all sides for about 5 minutes each time. Set aside.

Reduce the heat to medium, then add the leek, carrot, celery and bay leaf to the dish and cook for 8 minutes, or until softened and lightly golden. Add the garlic and cook for 30 seconds, or until fragrant.

Pour in the wine, then bring to the boil and cook for 1 minute. Stir in the stock, oregano, thyme and lemon zest strips, then add the shanks and any resting juices. Bring to the boil, reduce the heat, then cover and simmer for 1 hour. Take the lid off and cook for a further 30–45 minutes, or until the lamb is very tender but not falling off the bone. Remove the shanks and vegetables and cover to keep warm.

Increase the heat to high, bring the sauce to the boil and cook for 20 minutes, or until reduced slightly. Add the asparagus and peas and cook for 2 minutes, then scoop them out with a slotted spoon and add to the lamb and other vegetables. Reduce the heat to a simmer.

Whisk together the egg yolks, cream, lemon juice and sherry, then gradually stir into the sauce. Cook for 5 minutes, or until slightly thickened. Return the shanks and vegetables to the pan with the artichokes and cook for a few minutes to heat through. Discard the bay leaf and lemon zest strips, season to taste and serve with mash or rice.

In this dish, tender poached salt cod — a staple ingedient in the Basque region of Spain — is served on crispy, golden potatoes, topped with a piquant dressing. Follow the soaking instructions carefully to ensure the cod is tender and excess salt is removed.

bacalao with caper parsley dressing

4 x 150 g (5$^{1}/_{2}$ oz) bacalao (dried salt cod) portions,
   cut from the widest part of the fish (see Note)
3 evenly sized all-purpose potatoes, such as desiree
   or pontiac
185 ml (6 fl oz/$^{3}/_{4}$ cup) white wine
1 fresh bay leaf
olive oil, for deep-frying

caper parsley dressing
1 tablespoon baby capers in salt
1 guindilla chilli in vinegar, drained and finely chopped
2 tablespoons finely chopped red onion
3 tablespoons finely chopped flat-leaf (Italian) parsley
3 tablespoons finely chopped coriander (cilantro) leaves
2 garlic cloves, finely chopped
3 teaspoons sherry vinegar
2$^{1}/_{2}$ tablespoons extra virgin olive oil
large pinch of caster (superfine) sugar

Serves 4

Soak the cod in cold water in the refrigerator for 24 hours, changing the water several times.

About an hour before you wish to serve, wash the potatoes well and cut them into 1.5 cm ($^{5}/_{8}$ inch) thick slices, keeping the skin on. Cook in boiling water for 10 minutes, or until starting to become tender. Drain, rinse well, then pat dry with paper towels or a clean tea towel (dish towel). Set aside to dry completely.

Remove the cod from its soaking liquid and neatly trim if necessary. Half-fill a large, deep frying pan with water, add the wine and bay leaf and bring to the boil. Reduce to a low simmer, then add the cod and cook for 30–35 minutes, or until very tender but not falling apart.

Meanwhile, fill a deep-fryer or large heavy-based saucepan one-third full of oil and heat to 190°C (375°F), or until a cube of bread dropped into the oil browns in 10 seconds. Deep-fry the potato slices in batches for 8 minutes each time, or until crisp and golden — you will probably need to work in four batches. Drain on crumpled paper towels, sprinkle lightly with salt and keep warm in a low oven until serving.

While the potato is cooking, make the caper parsley dressing. Soak the capers in a small bowl of water for 10 minutes, then rinse, squeeze dry and finely chop. Put them in a bowl with the remaining dressing ingredients and mix well.

Lift the cod out of the cooking liquid using a slotted spatula, then drain on crumpled paper towels. Arrange a few warm potato slices on each serving plate, top with the cod portions, spoon the dressing over and serve.

Note: If you can't get pre-cut pieces of salt cod, soak larger pieces of fish, then cut them into 150 g (5$^{1}/_{2}$ oz) portions before cooking.

Warming and satisfying, this wintery hotpot is enlivened with a sharp picada —
a toasty nut, bread and herb paste stirred through just before serving to add extra
texture, flavour and aroma. The crackling adds crunch to the meltingly tender meat.

pork and lima bean hotpot with green picada and pork crackling

350 g (12 oz/1^1/$_2$ cups) dried lima beans (butterbeans)
1 kg (2 lb 4 oz) boneless pork belly
1 tablespoon olive oil
1 brown onion, chopped
1 large celery stalk, chopped
^{1}/$_2$ fennel bulb, cut into 2 cm (^{3}/$_4$ inch) cubes
2 garlic cloves, finely chopped
1 fresh bay leaf
1 teaspoon ground aniseed
375 ml (13 fl oz/1^1/$_2$ cups) white wine
500 g (1 lb 2 oz) white butifarra sausages, or other
    mild, fresh pork sausages (such as Italian-style
    pork and fennel)
700 g (1 lb 9 oz) piece of smoked pork hock
2 litres (70 fl oz) home-made or low-salt chicken stock
sliced or whole guindilla chillies in vinegar (optional),
    to garnish

green picada
10 almonds, toasted
1 slice well-toasted bread
2 garlic cloves
3 tablespoons fennel fronds
2 tablespoons chopped mint
3 handfuls flat-leaf (Italian) parsley
80 ml (2^1/$_2$ fl oz/^{1}/$_3$ cup) extra virgin olive oil
1^1/$_2$ tablespoons cider vinegar or sherry vinegar
^{1}/$_2$ teaspoon dry anis, or other dry aniseed liqueur

Serves 6–8

Rinse the beans and place in a large saucepan of water. Bring to the boil and cook for 2 minutes, then turn off the heat. Leave for 2 hours, then drain well.

Cut the top layer of fat and skin from the pork belly and reserve. Cut the meat into 4 cm (1^1/$_2$ inch) squares.

Heat the oil in a large flameproof casserole dish over medium–high heat. Add the pork meat and brown on all sides for 4–5 minutes, then remove. Add the onion, celery and fennel and cook for 6–8 minutes, or until lightly golden, stirring occasionally. Add the garlic, bay leaf and aniseed and stir for 1 minute, or until fragrant. Stir in the wine, bring to the boil and cook for 2 minutes.

Prick the sausages all over with a fork, then add them whole to the casserole dish, along with the browned pork belly, pork hock and stock. Bring to the boil. Reduce the heat, cover and simmer for 1^1/$_2$ hours. Add the beans and cook, uncovered, for a further 1 hour, or until the beans and meat are very tender.

Preheat the oven to 200°C (400°F/Gas 6). While the hotpot is simmering, make the crackling. Cut the reserved pork fat into 2 cm (^{3}/$_4$ inch) chunks, then scatter over a baking tray and sprinkle liberally with salt. Roast for 35–40 minutes, or until crisp and golden. Drain well on crumpled paper towels and set aside.

To make the green picada, put the almonds, toast, garlic, fennel fronds, mint and parsley in a food processor and blend to a rough paste. Stir in the oil, vinegar and anis. Set aside until ready to serve.

When the beans and meat are tender, remove all the solids from the hotpot. When cool enough to handle, strip the meat from the ham hock and slice the butifarra. Set aside. Bring the cooking liquid to the boil and cook for 20 minutes, or until thickened slightly. Add the solids back to the pan and cook for a further few minutes to heat through.

Serve the hotpot with the picada on the side for stirring in, and the crackling for sprinkling over, perhaps with a small bowl of tart, spicy guindilla chillies on the side for extra bite.

Usually I prefer to serve tuna fillets pink and rare, but with this dish a longer cooking time helps the flavours to permeate more deeply. During poaching, the tuna is completely submerged in oil, resulting in very tender fish.

oil-poached tuna with cherry tomatoes

24 cherry tomatoes, on the vine
   (about 500 g/1 lb 2 oz in total)
2 fresh bay leaves
6 garlic cloves, peeled
4 small dried, smoked red chillies, preferably
   red guindilla chillies if available
2 anchovies, finely chopped
1 large thyme sprig, chopped
$\frac{1}{2}$ teaspoon finely shredded lemon zest
$\frac{1}{2}$ teaspoon black peppercorns
$\frac{1}{2}$ teaspoon caster (superfine) sugar
750 ml (26 fl oz/3 cups) good-quality olive oil
4 x 200 g (7 oz) best-quality tuna steaks

Serves 4

Preheat the oven to 160°C (315°F/Gas 2–3). Snip the tomatoes off the vine, leaving a little stem attached for presentation, then sit them in a 20 x 30 cm (8 x 12 inch) baking dish (the dish should just be large enough to fit all the fish in a single layer). Add the bay leaves, garlic cloves, chillies, anchovies, thyme, lemon zest and peppercorns. Sprinkle over the sugar and season with salt. Pour the oil over and bake for 35 minutes, or until the tomatoes are slightly shrivelled and the garlic is softened.

Using a slotted spoon, remove the solids to a bowl, then cover and keep warm. Sit the tuna in a single layer in the oil and bake for 18–20 minutes, or until just cooked through.

Carefully lift the fish onto four serving plates using a spatula. Pile some of the tomato mixture on top and serve.

It is not unusual in Spanish cuisine to use chocolate to enrich and thicken savoury dishes. Here, dark grated chocolate is teamed with cinnamon and other warming spices in this fabulous wintery pie, topped with a crunchy cornmeal lid.

oxtail pie with cornmeal crust

2 tablespoons olive oil
2.5 kg (5 lb 8 oz) oxtail, cut into 3 cm (1¼ inch)
    thick pieces (ask your butcher to do this)
1 large red onion, chopped
2 carrots, cut into 2 cm (¾ inch) cubes
3 garlic cloves, finely chopped
1½ teaspoons ground cinnamon
pinch of ground cloves
3 teaspoons ground cumin
750 ml (26 fl oz) bottle Spanish red wine,
    such as tempranillo
800 g (1 lb 12 oz/3¼ cups) tin chopped tomatoes
1.5 litres (52 fl oz/6 cups) home-made or low-salt
    beef stock
2 tablespoons grated dark chocolate

cornmeal crust
125 g (4½ oz/1 cup) plain (all-purpose) flour
150 g (5½ oz/1 cup) fine cornmeal (polenta)
1 teaspoon salt
90 g (3¼ oz) lard or butter, frozen
4–5 tablespoons iced water
1 egg, lightly beaten with 2 teaspoons water

Serves 6–8

Heat the oil in a large saucepan or stockpot over medium–high heat and brown the oxtail well in two batches for 3–5 minutes on each side. Set aside.

Reduce the heat to medium, add the onion and carrot and cook for 15 minutes, or until golden, stirring occasionally. Add the garlic, cinnamon, cloves and cumin and cook for 1 minute, or until fragrant. Stir in the wine, tomato and stock, then put the oxtail back in the pan. Bring to the boil, then reduce the heat and simmer for 4¼ to 4½ hours, or until the oxtail is very tender, skimming off any scum that rises to the surface during cooking. Skim off all the excess fat.

Remove the oxtail and set aside to cool. Meanwhile, increase the heat and boil the sauce for 5 minutes, or until thickened slightly. When the oxtail is cool enough to handle, remove all the meat from the bones and stir it back into the sauce. Season to taste, allow to cool slightly, then refrigerate for 2 hours, or until cold.

Meanwhile, make the cornmeal crust. Put the flour, cornmeal and salt in a bowl. Grate the frozen lard over the top, then rub it into the flour with your fingertips until the mixture resembles fine breadcrumbs. Make a well in the centre. Pour in most of the water and mix with a flat-bladed knife until the pastry comes together in beads, adding a little more water if necessary. Gather together and flatten to a thick disc. It will still be a little sticky, but the cornmeal will absorb some of the liquid. Cover with plastic wrap and refrigerate for 1 hour.

Preheat the oven to 190°C (375°F/Gas 5). Stir the chocolate through the oxtail mixture, then pour into a deep, 20 x 30 cm (8 x 12 inch) or 2.5 litre (88 fl oz/10 cup capacity) ceramic baking dish and smooth the surface.

Roll the pastry out between two sheets of baking paper until 3 mm (⅛ inch) thick. Lift off the top sheet and invert the pastry onto the pie dish, then lift off the remaining sheet of baking paper. Press down around the pastry edges to help the crust adhere, then trim the edges to neaten it. Brush the pastry with beaten egg, then use the tip of a small sharp knife to pierce several air holes over the top. Bake for 1 hour, or until the crust is golden and the filling is hot. Delicious served with mashed potato and salad, or even just a salad.

This dish is loosely based on a simple Basque recipe in which fish is cooked in a sauce of its own juices, olive oil and parsley. Don't be daunted by the number of ingredients in this dressed-up green sauce — it is actually very easy.

almond-crusted hake with green sauce

4 x 200 g (7 oz) hake fillets, or other firm white fish fillets
seasoned plain (all-purpose) flour, for coating
2 eggs, lightly beaten
235 g (8^1/$_2$ oz/2^1/$_3$ cups) ground almonds
olive oil, for pan-frying
lemon wedges, to serve

broad bean purée
1.5 kg (3 lb 5 oz) broad (fava) beans in the pod,
    shelled, or 450 g (1 lb/3 cups) frozen broad
    (fava) beans, thawed
30 g (1 oz) butter
60 ml (2 fl oz/^{1}/$_4$ cup) cream (whipping)

green sauce
1^1/$_2$ tablespoons olive oil
2 garlic cloves, finely chopped
2 anchovies, very finely chopped
^{1}/$_2$ green capsicum (pepper), finely diced
4 spring onions (scallions), sliced
50 g (1^3/$_4$ oz/^{1}/$_3$ cup) blanched fresh peas,
    or thawed frozen peas
6 thin asparagus spears, cut into 3 cm (1^1/$_4$ inch)
    lengths on the diagonal
125 ml (4 fl oz/^{1}/$_2$ cup) home-made or low-salt
    chicken stock
1 tablespoon fino (dry) sherry
2 teaspoons sherry vinegar
1 tablespoon finely chopped green olives
1 tablespoon finely chopped mint
1 large handful flat-leaf (Italian) parsley, finely chopped

Serves 4

Lightly coat the fish fillets in seasoned flour, then dip into the beaten egg, allowing any excess to drip off. Press the fish into the ground almonds, then refrigerate, uncovered, until ready to cook.

To make the broad bean purée, cook the beans in a saucepan of boiling water for 8 minutes, or until very tender. Drain well. When cool enough to handle, slip them out of their skins. Put them in a saucepan with the butter and cream. Heat gently, then purée with a stick or hand blender until smooth. Season to taste and set aside.

Next, start making the green sauce. Heat the oil in a saucepan over medium–high heat. Add the garlic and anchovies and stir for 6 minutes, or until the garlic is lightly golden. Add the capsicum, spring onion, peas and asparagus and sauté for 5 minutes, or until the asparagus is just becoming tender. Remove from the pan and set aside (the green sauce must be finished just before serving to keep the flavours fresh). Keep the saucepan handy.

Heat 1 cm (^{1}/$_2$ inch) of oil in a large frying pan over medium heat. Add the fish and cook for 4–5 minutes on each side, or until the coating is golden and the fish is just cooked through. Drain on crumpled paper towels.

Meanwhile, gently reheat the broad bean purée, thinning it with a little extra cream if desired, and finish making the green sauce. Put the reserved saucepan back over high heat. Pour in the stock, sherry and sherry vinegar and bring to the boil for 4 minutes. Return the capsicum, pea and asparagus mixture back to the pan and stir in the olives, mint and parsley, tossing to coat well.

Put a dollop of broad bean purée on four serving plates, top with a piece of fish, spoon over the green sauce and serve.

Given the importance of sheep to the Spanish economy, it's not surprising Spaniards love lamb and are expert at cooking it. Here a tender leg of lamb is smothered in a golden crust of herbs, lemon, anchovies and garlic, then roasted to perfection.

roast lamb leg with garlic herb crust

garlic herb crust

1 whole head of garlic

60 ml (2 fl oz/1/4 cup) olive oil

1 teaspoon sea salt flakes

165 g (5³/4 oz/2 cups) large fresh breadcrumbs

1/2 teaspoon finely grated lemon zest

1¹/2 teaspoons finely chopped rosemary

1¹/2 teaspoons finely chopped thyme

1 handful flat-leaf (Italian) parsley, chopped

4 anchovies, finely chopped

2 kg (4 lb 8 oz) leg of lamb

1 onion, chopped

1 carrot, chopped

1 celery stalk, chopped

685 ml (23¹/2 fl oz/2³/4 cups) home-made or
    low-salt chicken stock

20 g (³/4 oz) butter

1 tablespoon plain (all-purpose) flour

1¹/2 tablespoons fino (dry) sherry

Serves 6

Preheat the oven to 190°C (375°F/Gas 5). To make the garlic herb crust, put the garlic in a saucepan and fill the pan with cold water. Bring to the boil over high heat and cook for 8–10 minutes, or until soft. Drain, leave until cool enough to handle, then slip the garlic cloves from their skins into a bowl. Add the oil and mash to a smooth paste. Mix in the salt, breadcrumbs, lemon zest, herbs and anchovies.

Press the crust over the top of the lamb, in an even layer. Sit the lamb on a wire rack. Put the onion, carrot and celery in a roasting tin and rest the rack on top. Pour in 500 ml (17 fl oz/2 cups) of the stock and bake for 1¹/2 hours, or until the lamb is cooked to your liking and the crust is golden. If the crust starts browning too quickly, place a sheet of foil over the top. When the lamb is done, remove it from the tin, cover lightly and set aside to rest for 20 minutes.

Strain the roasting juices into a cup with a pouring lip, pressing down on any solids to extract the juices. Melt the butter in a saucepan over high heat, stir in the flour and cook for 1 minute. Stir in the sherry, then slowly whisk in the pan juices and the remaining stock. Add any resting juices from the lamb and stir constantly, until the gravy boils and thickens. Season to taste.

Carve the lamb and serve with some of the crust and the gravy. Roasted vegetables such as potatoes, red capsicum (pepper), red onion and baby eggplant (aubergine) make a wonderful accompaniment.

postres

A fun play on that famous chilled Spanish soup, this sweet, refreshing dessert soup is garnished with 'croutons' made from creamy frozen yoghurt, and scattered with finely diced 'greens' in the form of kiwi fruit, grapes and mint ...

strawberry gazpacho with frozen yoghurt

frozen yoghurt

375 g (13 oz/1½ cups) thick sheep's milk yoghurt

2 tablespoons milk

40 g (1½ oz/⅓ cup) icing (confectioners') sugar

2 teaspoons natural vanilla extract

strawberry purée

750 g (1 lb 10 oz/5 cups) very ripe, sweet
    strawberries, hulled

30 g (1 oz/¼ cup) sifted icing (confectioners')
    sugar, or to taste

1 teaspoon sherry vinegar

2 tablespoons oloroso sherry

2 kiwi fruit

12 seedless green grapes, halved lengthways

3 tablespoons finely diced honeydew melon

6 finely diced strawberries

1 tablespoon tiny mint leaves or finely shredded mint

Serves 4

To make the frozen yoghurt, whisk together the yoghurt, milk, icing sugar and vanilla extract until smooth. Line a 20 cm (8 inch) square shallow dish with two long strips of plastic wrap so that the edges overhang on each side. Pour the yoghurt mixture in and smooth the surface. Pull the plastic wrap over to cover, then freeze for 4 hours, or until set.

Meanwhile, make the strawberry purée. Put the strawberries and icing sugar in a food processor and blend to a purée, then strain through a fine sieve. Stir through the sherry vinegar and sherry and chill for 2–3 hours.

Peel the kiwi fruit, cut them into quarters, and trim off the seeds with a sharp knife. Finely dice the flesh.

Divide the strawberry purée among four shallow bowls. Slice the yoghurt into 1.5 cm (⅝ inch) cubes and scatter them over the top, along with the kiwi fruit, grapes, melon and strawberries. Garnish with mint and serve immediately.

Many Spanish desserts and cakes are rich in egg yolks. The whites are often used in *turron* or nougat, but when I think egg whites I think meringue! Chocolate and cinnamon are key Spanish flavours in this layered cake of chewy meringue and dark, silky mousse.

hazelnut meringue cake with choc cinnamon mousse

mousse

600 ml (21 fl oz) cream (whipping)

1 teaspoon ground cinnamon

300 g (10^1/2 oz) good-quality dark chocolate, finely grated

hazelnut meringue

6 large egg whites

145 g (5^1/4 oz/^{2}/3 cup) caster (superfine) sugar

1 teaspoon natural vanilla extract

125 g (4^1/2 oz/1 cup) icing (confectioners') sugar, sifted

30 g (1 oz/^{1}/4 cup) plain (all-purpose) flour

280 g (10 oz/2 cups) whole hazelnuts, toasted and finely ground

topping

40 g (1^1/2 oz/^{1}/3 cup) icing (confectioners') sugar

2 tablespoons unsweetened dark cocoa powder

1^1/2 teaspoons ground cinnamon

Serves 10–12

To make the mousse, pour 250 ml (9 fl oz/1 cup) of the cream into a saucepan, sprinkle with the cinnamon and place over medium heat. Allow the cream to heat until just below boiling point, then take it off the heat and set aside to infuse for 10 minutes. Strain into a clean pan through a fine sieve. Stir in the grated chocolate until melted (briefly put the pan back over very low heat if necessary), then cool to room temperature. Whip the remaining cream well, then fold it through the chocolate mixture. Cover and refrigerate for 2 hours, or until firm enough to spread.

Preheat the oven to 140°C (275°F/Gas 1), and line three Swiss roll (jelly roll) tins or baking trays with baking paper.

To make the hazelnut meringue, beat the egg whites with an electric beater until soft peaks form. With the motor still running, gradually add the caster sugar and vanilla extract and beat to stiff peaks. Mix the icing sugar, flour and ground hazelnuts together in a small bowl, then fold in two large spoonfuls of the meringue until well combined. Gently fold the nut mixture back into the rest of the egg white until well combined, being careful not to beat out the air.

Spoon one-third of the mixture into the centre of each baking tin, then smooth out into a rectangle about 18 x 25 cm (7 x 10 inches) in size. Bake for 1 hour, or until dry on top. Remove from the oven, allow to cool in the tins, then turn the meringues out and carefully peel off the baking paper.

To assemble the cake, put one meringue layer on a serving dish, then spread over half the mousse (if the mousse has become too firm just whisk it with a fork until it softens up again). Top with another meringue layer and spread with the remaining mousse. Top with the final meringue layer, then cover with plastic wrap and refrigerate for at least a few hours, or overnight. The meringue will soften slightly, making the cake easier to slice.

When ready to serve, sift the topping ingredients into a bowl, then sift the mixture over the cake. If serving the cake whole, you might like to trim the edges to neaten them. Otherwise, serve the cake cut into neat squares, perhaps with some lightly whipped cream.

Although quite similar to French toast, these popular bread fritters are usually eaten as a dessert rather than for breakfast. Although if you wanted to have them for breakfast, who's to stop you?

raisin torrijas with honey and walnuts

4 thick slices day-old raisin brioche,
    or other good-quality raisin bread
2 eggs
125 ml (4 fl oz/^{1}/2 cup) cream (whipping)
2 teaspoons caster (superfine) sugar
^{1}/2 teaspoon natural vanilla extract
mild vegetable oil, for pan-frying
20 g (^{3}/4 oz) butter
160 g (5^1/2 oz/scant ^{1}/2 cup) honey
1 tablespoon manzanilla sherry
35 g (1^1/4 oz/^{1}/3 cup) walnuts, toasted
    and roughly chopped

Serves 4

Cut the brioche slices into 3 cm (1^1/4 inch) wide fingers. Whisk together the eggs, cream, sugar and vanilla extract and pour into a non-metallic dish.

Put the brioche fingers in the egg mixture and turn to coat well. Leave to soak for 10 minutes.

Pour enough oil into a large frying pan to cover the base by 5 mm (^{1}/4 inch), then add the butter and place over medium–high heat. In two batches, lift the brioche fingers out of the egg mixture, allowing the excess to drip off, then fry for 2 minutes on each side, or until golden. Drain on crumpled paper towels.

Meanwhile, combine the honey, sherry and walnuts in a small saucepan and leave over low heat until the honey melts.

Divide the brioche fingers among four serving plates and spoon a little of the honey and walnut sauce over the top. Wonderful with vanilla ice cream.

Sangria, the celebrated Spanish drink, is made even more refreshing when churned into an icy-cold granita and served over fruit. It is especially spectacular dished up with ripe cherries and blood oranges, when in season.

sangria granita

500 ml (17 fl oz/2 cups) red wine, preferably Spanish
125 ml (4 fl oz/1/2 cup) strained, freshly squeezed
    orange juice
60 ml (2 fl oz/1/4 cup) strained, freshly squeezed
    lemon juice
375 ml (13 fl oz/11/2 cups) lemonade
60 ml (2 fl oz/1/4 cup) brandy
1/4 teaspoon ground cinnamon
21/2 tablespoons caster (superfine) sugar, or to taste
fruit of your choice (optional), to serve

Serves 6–8

Pour the wine, orange juice, lemon juice, lemonade and brandy into a bowl. Add the cinnamon and stir in the sugar until the sugar has dissolved. Pour into a shallow 1.5 litre (52 fl oz/6 cup capacity) freezer-friendly container and freeze for 2 hours, or until the mixture is starting to freeze around the edges.

Scrape the frozen edges back into the mixture with a fork. Repeat every 30 minutes for about 3 hours, or until evenly sized ice crystals have formed. If you are preparing the granita ahead of time, store it in the freezer and scrape once again just before serving. Serve in squat glasses over fruit, if desired.

Polvorones are a Spanish shortbread biscuit (cookie) flavoured with aniseed, but here the shortbread is used as a pastry case. Filled with thick custard spiked with cider and topped with caramelized apple, these rich tarts are a sublime autumn dessert.

polvorones with apple and cider custard

cider custard

375 ml (13 fl oz/1¹/₂ cups) cream (whipping)
125 ml (4 fl oz/¹/₂ cup) milk
8 egg yolks
60 ml (2 fl oz/¹/₄ cup) sweet Spanish *sidra,*
   or other sweet alcoholic apple cider
80 g (2³/₄ oz/¹/₃ cup) caster (superfine) sugar
1¹/₂ teaspoons natural vanilla extract
2 tablespoons plain (all-purpose) flour
1¹/₂ tablespoons cornflour (cornstarch)

pastry

250 g (9 oz/2 cups) plain (all-purpose) flour
1 teaspoon whole aniseeds
40 g (1¹/₂ oz/¹/₄ cup) pine nuts
60 g (2¹/₄ oz/¹/₂ cup) icing (confectioners') sugar
200 g (7 oz) unsalted butter, chilled and cut into cubes
1 egg yolk
1 teaspoon natural vanilla extract
2 teaspoons oloroso sherry

caramelized apple

30 g (1 oz) unsalted butter
8 small crisp, sweet apples (such as fuji),
   peeled, cored and cut into eighths
100 g (3¹/₂ oz/¹/₂ cup) soft brown sugar
80 ml (2¹/₂ fl oz/¹/₃ cup) sweet Spanish *sidra,*
   or other sweet alcoholic apple cider
80 ml (2¹/₂ fl oz/¹/₃ cup) clear apple juice
80 ml (2¹/₂ fl oz/¹/₃ cup) cream (whipping)

Makes 8

To make the cider custard, pour the cream and milk into a saucepan and just bring to the boil. Meanwhile, whisk together the egg yolks, cider, sugar, vanilla, flour and cornflour in a heatproof bowl. Gradually whisk in the hot cream mixture until smooth, then pour into a clean, heavy-based saucepan and place over low heat. Using a balloon whisk, stir continuously for 15 minutes, or until the mixture is thick and smooth and clearly holds a 'ribbon' shape when drizzled from the whisk onto the custard. Allow to cool slightly, then cover with plastic wrap and refrigerate for at least 4 hours, or until completely cold.

To make the pastry, put the flour, aniseeds, pine nuts and icing sugar in a food processor with a pinch of salt. Process until the nuts are finely chopped, then add the butter and pulse until the mixture forms crumbs. Put the egg yolk, vanilla extract and sherry in a bowl and mix together well. Using a flat-bladed knife and a cutting action, mix the liquid into the flour until it forms clumps. Gather together into a ball, wrap in plastic wrap and refrigerate for 1 hour.

Divide the dough into eight equal portions, then roll each one out between two sheets of baking paper to 5 mm (¹/₄ inch) thick. Remove the top layers of paper and invert the pastry over eight 10 cm (4 inch) individual tart tins with removable bases. Fit the pastry into the tins, trim the edges and freeze for 1 hour. Save any leftover pastry for making into shortbread biscuits (cookies).

Preheat the oven to 180°C (350°F/Gas 4). Bake the tart shells for 15 minutes, or until lightly golden and firm to the touch. Remove from the oven and allow to cool completely before releasing them from the tins.

While the tart shells are cooling, prepare the caramelized apple. Melt the butter in a large frying pan over medium–high heat and sauté the apple for 15 minutes, or until lightly golden — if your pan isn't quite large enough you may need to work in two batches. Remove the apple from the pan and stir in the sugar, cider, apple juice and cream. Stir until the sugar has dissolved, then bring to the boil and cook for 5 minutes. Mix the apple through, reduce the heat to medium and cook for 10 minutes, or until the apple is soft but not falling apart, and the sauce is golden and glazy. Allow to cool slightly.

Fill the tart shells with the custard, top with the warm apple and serve at once, perhaps with a glass of warm spiced *sidra* (see page 31).

In this recipe, cubes of sponge cake are drizzled with Licor 43 — a Spanish liqueur tasting of orange and vanilla — then layered with a refreshing orange and Cava jelly, creamy vanilla custard and ripe peaches to create a light, zippy trifle.

tipsy gypsy trifle

cava and orange jelly

250 ml (9 fl oz/1 cup) strained, freshly
    squeezed orange juice

500 ml (17 fl oz/2 cups) Cava or sparkling white wine

2 tablespoons caster (superfine) sugar

5 teaspoons powdered gelatine

custard

1 vanilla bean

250 ml (9 fl oz/1 cup) milk

375 ml (13 fl oz/1 1/2 cups) cream (whipping)

6 egg yolks

55 g (2 oz/1/4 cup) caster (superfine) sugar

1 tablespoon cornflour (cornstarch)

200 g (7 oz) day-old sponge cake, cut into
    2 cm (3/4 inch) cubes

60 ml (2 fl oz/1/4 cup) manzanilla sherry

60 ml (2 fl oz/1/4 cup) Licor 43, or other
    orange-flavoured liqueur

60 ml (2 fl oz/1/4 cup) strained, freshly
    squeezed orange juice

4 very ripe (or bottled) peaches, sliced

Serves 8

To make the Cava and orange jelly, put the orange juice, Cava and sugar in a saucepan over low heat until just hot, stirring to dissolve the sugar. Remove from the heat. Pour one-quarter of the hot liquid into a small bowl with a pouring lip, sprinkle over the gelatine and whisk with a fork until smooth. Stir back into the hot liquid and stir constantly until dissolved. Pour into a 1 litre (35 fl oz/4 cup capacity) container, allow to cool slightly, then cover and refrigerate for 6 hours, or until set.

To make the custard, split the vanilla bean down the middle, scrape out the seeds, then put the pod and seeds in a saucepan with the milk and cream. Place over low heat and bring to just below the boil. Turn off the heat and allow to infuse for 15 minutes.

Put the egg yolks, sugar and cornflour in a saucepan and whisk to combine. Pour in the hot cream mixture, whisking until smooth, then place over very low heat and stir continuously with a metal spoon for about 8 minutes, or until thickened. Remove from the heat, discard the vanilla bean pods, then press a sheet of plastic wrap onto the surface of the custard to prevent a skin forming. Allow to cool slightly, then refrigerate for 5 hours, or until completely cold.

Divide the sponge cake cubes among eight individual 420 ml (14 1/2 fl oz/ 1 2/3 cup capacity) glass bowls, or sit them in one large bowl. Combine the sherry, liqueur and orange juice and drizzle over the sponge. Sit the peach slices over the top, then dollop the custard over. Roughly chop the jelly and layer it over the custard. Refrigerate for at least 2 hours for the flavours to develop before serving.

I love rice pudding, especially Spanish style with a hint of cinnamon and lemon, but it can be a little heavy at the end of a meal. This version is aerated with whipped cream, then chilled and set with gelatine. It is a delightful summer treat served with fruit.

arroz con leche mousse with red fruit compôte

rice mousse

600 ml (21 fl oz) milk

110 g (3³/₄ oz/¹/₂ cup) Calasparra or paella rice

1 strip lemon zest

1 cinnamon stick

¹/₂ teaspoon natural vanilla extract

55 g (2 oz/¹/₄ cup) caster (superfine) sugar

2 teaspoons powdered gelatine

almond or other mild-flavoured oil, for brushing

170 ml (5¹/₂ fl oz/²/₃ cup) cream (whipping)

red fruit compôte

440 g (15¹/₂ oz/3¹/₂ cups) mixed seasonal red fruits, such as cherries, plums, red grapes, strawberries and raspberries

1¹/₂ tablespoons icing (confectioners') sugar

2 tablespoons Licor 43, or other orange-flavoured liqueur

¹/₄ teaspoon lemon juice

Serves 6

Start by making the rice mousse. Pour 500 ml (17 fl oz/2 cups) of the milk into a saucepan, add the rice, lemon zest, cinnamon stick, vanilla extract, sugar and a pinch of salt and stir over medium–high heat until the sugar has dissolved. Bring just to the boil, then reduce the heat and gently simmer for 30–35 minutes, stirring occasionally, or until the rice is tender but not mushy.

Put the remaining milk in a small saucepan and bring to the boil. Remove from the heat and sprinkle over the gelatine. When it becomes spongy, whisk until smooth and completely dissolved, then stir into the rice mixture. Remove from the heat, spread the rice onto a large baking tray and allow to cool slightly, then refrigerate for 30 minutes, or until cool. Discard the cinnamon stick and lemon zest.

Brush six 125 ml (4 fl oz/¹/₂ cup) moulds lightly with oil. Spoon the cooled rice into a bowl. Whip the cream to firm peaks, then fold it into the rice. Spoon the rice mousse into the moulds, without filling all the way to the top, then refrigerate for 2 hours, or until set.

While the rice mousse is setting, make the red fruit compôte. Dice or slice any larger pieces of fruit and place all the fruit in a bowl. Combine the icing sugar, liqueur and lemon juice and stir into the fruit. Cover and leave to sit at room temperature, stirring occasionally, until ready to serve. Unmould the rice onto six serving plates and serve with the red fruit compôte.

This dessert was inspired by two Spanish sweets: *intxaursalsa,* made from walnuts, and *turron*, a type of nougat based on toasted nuts and sugar. I love a piece of sweet *turron* with coffee, but here the flavours are combined — no need to boil the kettle!

frozen walnut turron with coffee syrup

walnut toffee
100 g (3^1/$_2$ oz/1 cup) walnuts, toasted
145 g (5^1/$_4$ oz/^{2}/$_3$ cup) caster (superfine) sugar

3 eggs, separated
2 tablespoons caster (superfine) sugar
60 ml (2 fl oz/^{1}/$_4$ cup) walnut liqueur, such as
    Nocello, Licor de Nuez or Licor de Nogado
1^1/$_2$ teaspoons natural vanilla extract
pinch of caster (superfine) sugar, extra
310 ml (10^3/$_4$ fl oz/1 ^{1}/$_4$ cups) cream (whipping)

coffee syrup
2 teaspoons instant coffee granules
115 g (4 oz/^{1}/$_2$ cup) caster (superfine) sugar

Serves 8

Line a baking tray with baking paper and spread the walnuts over the top, in a single layer.

To make the walnut toffee, put the sugar in a saucepan with 125 ml (4 fl oz/ ^{1}/$_2$ cup) of water and stir with a metal spoon over medium heat until the sugar has dissolved. Bring to the boil and allow to boil for about 10 minutes, without stirring, until dark golden. Carefully pour the mixture over the walnuts and leave for 30 minutes, or until set.

Meanwhile, using electric beaters, beat the egg yolks with the sugar, walnut liqueur and 1 teaspoon of the vanilla extract until very pale and creamy — this should take about 10 minutes.

In a separate bowl, whisk the egg whites with a pinch of sugar, using electric beaters, until firm peaks form.

Break the walnut toffee into small pieces, then put them in a food processor and blend until finely crushed. Lightly whip the cream. Stir the crushed toffee into the egg yolk mixture, then carefully but thoroughly fold in the cream, then the beaten egg whites. Pour into a 10 x 21 cm (4 x 8^1/$_4$ inch) loaf (bar) tin and smooth the surface. Freeze for 4 hours, or until firm.

Nearer to serving time, make the coffee syrup. Put the coffee granules and sugar in a small saucepan with 250 ml (9 fl oz/1 cup) of water and stir over medium heat until the sugar has dissolved. Bring to the boil and cook for 13 minutes, or until syrupy.

To serve, briefly dip the base of the loaf tin in hot water and invert the frozen *turron* onto a serving dish. Drizzle with a little coffee syrup and serve.

Amazingly rich, dark and velvety smooth, Pedro Ximénez sherry has gained international fame. It is now available from most good wine stores, so you too can be fortunate enough to always have a bottle at hand — not that it will last long once you taste it!

pears poached in pedro ximénez sherry

145 g (5¼ oz/⅔ cup) caster (superfine) sugar
2 long, wide strips of lemon zest
1 cinnamon stick
375 ml (13 fl oz/1½ cups) Pedro Ximénez sherry
6 firm pears, such as beurre bosc, peeled, stems intact
vanilla ice cream or lightly whipped cream, to serve
100 g (3½ oz) best-quality bitter dark chocolate
    (optional), to serve

Serves 6

Put the sugar, lemon zest and cinnamon stick in a large saucepan with 750 ml (26 fl oz/3 cups) of water. Stir over medium–high heat until the sugar has dissolved, then allow to come to the boil. Add the sherry and whole pears and allow to come to the boil again. Reduce the heat, then cover and simmer for 50 minutes to 1 hour, or until the pears are tender, carefully turning them now and then — the actual cooking time will depend on the firmness of the pears.

Take the pan off the heat and allow the pears to cool, then stand them in a deep dish just big enough to hold them all upright. Pour the cooking liquid over the pears and refrigerate overnight.

Lift the pears out of the liquid and pour the liquid into a saucepan. Bring to the boil and allow to boil for 25 minutes, or until it becomes a syrupy glaze.

Divide the pears among six serving dishes, drizzle with the warm syrup and serve with vanilla ice cream or lightly whipped cream. If you're using the chocolate, cut or break it into shards and serve alongside the pears — with a glass of Pedro Ximénez sherry, of course!

Almond cakes in various forms are popular all over Spain. Gooey but not too sweet, this super-moist version is delicious served with a scoop of silky, citrus ice cream melting into the cake still warm from the oven.

warm almond cake with citrus ice cream

citrus ice cream

1 vanilla bean
250 ml (9 fl oz/1 cup) cream (whipping)
500 ml (17 fl oz/2 cups) milk
2 teaspoons finely grated lemon zest
2 teaspoons finely grated orange zest
8 egg yolks
170 g (6 oz/$3/4$ cup) caster (superfine) sugar
80 ml ($2^1/2$ fl oz/$1/3$ cup) strained, freshly squeezed
    lemon juice
80 ml ($2^1/2$ fl oz/$1/3$ cup) strained, freshly squeezed
    orange juice

almond cake

200 g (7 oz) unsalted butter, chilled and cut into cubes
1 teaspoon natural vanilla extract
1 teaspoon finely grated lemon zest
1 teaspoon finely grated orange zest
310 g (11 oz/$2^1/2$ cups) icing (confectioners')
    sugar, sifted
4 eggs, separated
125 ml (4 fl oz/$1/2$ cup) milk
400 g (14 oz/$2^2/3$ cups) almonds, lightly toasted,
    then finely ground
icing (confectioners') sugar, for dusting

Serves 8–10

To make the citrus ice cream, split the vanilla bean down the middle, scrape out the seeds, then put the pod and seeds in a saucepan with the cream, milk, lemon zest and orange zest over medium heat. Slowly bring just to the boil, then remove from the heat and leave to infuse for 15 minutes.

In a bowl, whisk together the egg yolks and sugar, then pour in the cream mixture, whisking continuously. Stir in the lemon juice and orange juice. Pour into a clean saucepan, place over medium–low heat and stir for 25 minutes, or until the mixture coats the back of a spoon. Allow to cool slightly, pour into a clean bowl, then cover and refrigerate for $2^1/2$ hours, or until cold. Strain, then freeze in an ice cream machine according to the manufacturer's instructions.

If you don't have an ice cream machine, pour the mixture into a shallow metal tin and freeze for 2–3 hours, or until the mixture is just frozen around the edges. Working quickly, transfer the mixture to a large bowl and beat with electric beaters until smooth. Pour the mixture back into the tray and refreeze. Repeat this step three times. For the final freezing, transfer the mixture to an airtight container and cover the surface with a piece of baking paper and a lid.

While the ice cream is freezing, make the almond cake. Preheat the oven to 180°C (350°F/Gas 4), and line a 23 cm (9 inch), non-stick cake tin with baking paper. Using electric beaters, mix the butter, vanilla extract, lemon zest, orange zest and 250 g (9 oz/2 cups) of the icing sugar until pale and creamy. Gradually beat in the egg yolks until thoroughly combined. Add the milk and ground almonds and mix well.

Using electric beaters, beat the egg whites in another bowl with the remaining icing sugar and a pinch of salt until firm peaks form. Fold a large spoonful of the egg white through the cake batter, then carefully fold through the rest. Pour into the lined cake tin, smooth the top and bake for 30 minutes, then cover with foil and bake for a further 20–30 minutes, or until the top is dark golden and springs back when pressed.

Allow to cool slightly in the tin, then turn the warm cake out, dust with icing sugar, cut into slices and serve warm with a scoop of citrus ice cream.

Buñuelos are usually deep fried, like the tapas dish on page 24, but in this sweet interpretation of the savoury classic they are baked in the oven then allowed to cool, and the crisp shells filled with rich orange curd and whipped cream.

sweet buñuelos with orange curd

orange curd

80 ml (2^1/$_2$ fl oz/^{1}/$_3$ cup) strained, freshly squeezed orange juice

1^1/$_2$ teaspoons finely grated orange zest

80 g (2^3/$_4$ oz/^{1}/$_3$ cup) caster (superfine) sugar

100 g (3^1/$_2$ oz) unsalted butter, chopped

5 egg yolks, lightly beaten

sweet buñuelos

60 ml (2 fl oz/^{1}/$_4$ cup) extra virgin olive oil

^{1}/$_2$ teaspoon finely grated orange zest

1 teaspoon caster (superfine) sugar

60 g (2^1/$_4$ oz/^{1}/$_2$ cup) plain (all-purpose) flour, sifted

2 large eggs, at room temperature, lightly beaten

cream filling

170 ml (5^1/$_2$ fl oz/^{2}/$_3$ cup) cream (whipping)

1 teaspoon natural vanilla extract

1 tablespoon icing (confectioners') sugar

cinnamon sugar

1^1/$_2$ tablespoons icing (confectioners') sugar, combined with 1 teaspoon ground cinnamon

Serves 6

To make the orange curd, put the orange juice, orange zest, sugar and butter in a small saucepan and stir constantly over medium heat until the sugar has dissolved. Remove from the heat and stir in the egg yolks, mixing well. Put the pan back over very low heat and stir constantly for 8 minutes, or until the curd is thick, glossy and easily coats the back of a spoon — do not let it boil or it may split. Set aside to cool, then cover and refrigerate until ready to use.

Preheat the oven to 220°C (425°F/Gas 7). To make the sweet buñuelos, put 90 ml (3 fl oz) of water in a small heavy-based saucepan with the oil, orange zest, sugar and a pinch of salt and stir until the sugar has dissolved. Bring just to the boil over high heat, then take off the heat and immediately tip in the flour, stirring for 1 minute, or until the mixture forms a smooth paste and comes away from the side of the pan. Place back over medium heat and cook, stirring vigorously and continuously, for 5 minutes — a 'film' should start to coat the bottom of the pan, but if the oil starts to separate, the mixture is overheated and you will need to start again.

Remove from the heat, allow to cool slightly, then gradually mix in the eggs with a wooden spoon until very well combined, then continue beating for a few minutes until the mixture is thick, glossy and smooth.

Line two baking trays with baking paper. Spoon three 4 cm (1^1/$_2$ inch) wide mounds onto each baking tray, 5 cm (2 inches) apart. Bake for 10 minutes, or until puffed, then reduce the oven temperature to 180°C (350°F/Gas 4) and cook for 20 minutes, or until crisp and golden. Remove from the oven and pierce a small hole in each base to let the steam escape. Cool on a cake rack.

Meanwhile, make the cream filling. Put the cream, vanilla extract and icing sugar in a bowl and whip to soft peaks using electric beaters.

Split the puffs in half. Dollop the orange curd over the bases, then the cream filling. Sit the lids on top, then sift the cinnamon sugar over and serve at once.

Note: Choux pastry can be temperamental so it is important to measure the ingredients precisely and to follow the method carefully.

Crisp on the outside, with a lusciously creamy custard centre, *leche frita* — literally 'fried milk' — is pure comfort food. This fancy-pants version is studded with dark chocolate and drizzled with a heady cinnamon syrup.

chocolate chip leche frita

leche frita
1 vanilla bean
750 ml (26 fl oz/3 cups) milk
1 strip orange zest
60 g (2¼ oz/½ cup) cornflour (cornstarch)
5 egg yolks
115 g (4 oz/½ cup) caster (superfine) sugar
60 g (2¼ oz) good-quality dark chocolate, chopped
vegetable oil, for deep-frying
plain (all-purpose) flour, for coating
2 egg whites, lightly beaten
dry breadcrumbs, for coating
vanilla ice cream (optional), to serve

cinnamon syrup
115 g (4 oz/½ cup) caster (superfine) sugar
½ teaspoon ground cinnamon
1 teaspoon natural vanilla extract
2 tablespoons Pedro Ximénez sherry

Serves 6–8

First, make the *leche frita*. Split the vanilla bean down the middle, scrape out the seeds, then put the pod and seeds in a saucepan along with the milk and orange zest. Bring to the boil over medium–high heat, then take the pan off the heat.

In a heatproof bowl, whisk together the cornflour, egg yolks and sugar, then pour in the hot milk, whisking continuously until the mixture is thickened and smooth. Pour into a clean saucepan and stir over low heat for about 15 minutes to cook the cornflour, so the custard doesn't taste chalky. Take off the heat and allow to cool to room temperature, then remove the vanilla bean pods and orange zest. Stir in the chopped chocolate — the mixture should be sufficiently cooled by now that the chocolate chunks don't melt.

Line a 17 x 27 cm (6½ x 10¾ inch) dish with baking paper so that it overhangs on all sides. Spread the custard mixture into the dish, smoothing the top. Freeze for 4 hours, or until frozen.

Meanwhile, make the cinnamon syrup. Put the sugar, cinnamon and vanilla extract in a saucepan with 250 ml (9 fl oz/1 cup) of water. Stir over high heat until the sugar has dissolved, then allow the mixture to come to the boil. Reduce the heat and simmer for 20 minutes, or until syrupy. Remove from the heat and stir in the sherry.

Heat 1 cm (½ inch) of oil in a large, heavy-based frying pan over medium–high heat. Lift the frozen custard out of the dish using the overhanging flaps of baking paper as handles, then cut into six or eight roughly square pieces. Lightly coat them in flour, dip them into the egg whites, allowing any excess to drip off, then coat them in breadcrumbs.

Working quickly, fry the *leche frita* in several batches for 2 minutes on each side, or until they are golden and the custard is heated through. Drain on crumpled paper towels, then place on serving plates and drizzle with the cinnamon syrup. Serve with vanilla ice cream, if desired.

Saffron is widely used in Spanish cooking, but isn't usually associated with desserts. It is wonderful combined with vanilla, lemon and cream in this luscious panna cotta accompanied by a fresh little fruit salad of citrus fruits, pineapple and passionfruit.

saffron panna cotta

1 vanilla bean
125 ml (4 fl oz/$\frac{1}{2}$ cup) milk
435 ml (15$\frac{1}{4}$ fl oz/1$\frac{3}{4}$ cups) cream (whipping)
large pinch of saffron threads
1 teaspoon finely grated lemon zest
145 g (5$\frac{1}{4}$ oz/$\frac{2}{3}$ cup) caster (superfine) sugar
2$\frac{1}{2}$ teaspoons powdered gelatine
almond or mild-flavoured vegetable oil, for brushing

1 pink grapefruit
2 blood oranges
$\frac{1}{3}$ small pineapple, skin and core removed
2 panama passionfruit, cut in half
1 small handful baby mint (optional)
icing (confectioners') sugar, to taste

Serves 4

Split the vanilla bean down the middle, scrape out the seeds, then put the pod and seeds in a saucepan with the milk, cream, saffron, lemon zest and sugar. Stir over medium heat until the sugar has dissolved. Allow to come just below the boil, then reduce the heat and simmer for 2 minutes. Remove from the heat and leave to infuse for 10 minutes. Place back over the heat and just bring to the boil again, then remove from the heat.

Put the gelatine in a small bowl and whisk in 60 ml (2 fl oz/$\frac{1}{4}$ cup) of the hot milk mixture until smooth. Pour the mixture back into the saucepan and whisk until the gelatine has completely dissolved. Strain the mixture into a pitcher. Lightly oil four 125 ml (4 fl oz/$\frac{1}{2}$ cup) moulds, then pour in the milk mixture and allow to cool slightly. Cover with plastic wrap and refrigerate for 4 hours, or until set. The panna cotta should still be slightly wobbly.

Meanwhile, cut the ends off the grapefruit and oranges, then sit them flat on a cutting board. Using a sharp knife, slice off all the skin and pith, all the way around. Holding one piece of fruit over a bowl, carefully cut down either side of each citrus segment and remove them, placing them in the bowl and squeezing any juice from the membranes over the segments. Segment the remaining citrus in the same way.

Cut the pineapple into thin slices and add them to the citrus. Scoop the passionfruit pulp into the bowl, add the mint leaves if desired and gently mix together. Sweeten with a little icing sugar, if needed.

Briefly dip the base of the moulds in hot water, and run a knife around the inside edge of each mould to help loosen the panna cotta if necessary. Invert onto four serving plates, spoon the fruit around and serve.

It is no wonder that a country with such an affinity with almonds produces excellent marzipan. Those who find marzipan too strong will be pleasantly surprised by the subtle sweetness of the Spanish version, all gooey and dotted through the pudding.

fig and marzipan bread and butter pudding

8 dried figs
100 ml (3^1/$_2$ fl oz) Pedro Ximénez or oloroso sherry
350 g (12 oz) day-old brioche
100 g (3^1/$_2$ oz) unsalted butter
150 g (5^1/$_2$ oz) marzipan (preferably Spanish), diced
8 egg yolks
375 ml (13 fl oz/1^1/$_2$ cups) milk
500 ml (17 fl oz/2 cups) cream (whipping)
115 g (4 oz/^{1}/$_2$ cup) caster (superfine) sugar
1^1/$_2$ teaspoons natural vanilla extract
whipped cream, to serve

topping
45 g (1^1/$_2$ oz/^{1}/$_2$ cup) flaked almonds
2 tablespoons caster (superfine) sugar
2 teaspoons ground cinnamon

Serves 8

Preheat the oven to 160°C (315°F/Gas 2–3). Chop the figs and put them in a small saucepan with the sherry. Bring to the boil, cook for 1 minute, then reduce the heat and simmer, stirring occasionally, for 10 minutes, or until the liquid has evaporated.

Thickly slice the brioche. Butter each slice on both sides, then cut into 3 cm (1^1/$_4$ inch) cubes. Add them to the figs with the diced marzipan and toss together well. Tip the mixture into a buttered 20 x 30 cm (8 x 12 inch) baking dish and spread out evenly.

In a bowl, whisk together the eggs, milk, cream, sugar and vanilla extract. Pour it over the bread, then press the bread down into the liquid and leave to rest for 20 minutes to help the bread soak up the liquid.

Combine the topping ingredients, then sprinkle the mixture over the pudding and bake for 40 minutes, or until slightly puffed and golden. Serve warm with whipped cream.

Spanish-blooded or not, coffee aficionados will appreciate this wonderful jelly topped with sweetened whipped cream. Use your favourite coffee and make it as strong as you like — especially if you plan to stay up late! If not, opt for a decaffeinated blend.

cafe con leche jelly

500 ml (17 fl oz/2 cups) freshly brewed coffee
2 tablespoons soft brown sugar, or to taste
2 teaspoons powdered gelatine
1 tablespoon coffee liqueur
125 ml (4 fl oz/1/2 cup) cream (whipping)
1 tablespoon icing (confectioners') sugar
1 teaspoon natural vanilla extract
ground cinnamon, for sprinkling

Serves 6

Put the coffee and sugar in a small saucepan over medium–high heat. Stir until the sugar has dissolved, then bring to the boil. Remove from the heat and pour 60 ml (2 fl oz/1/4 cup) of the hot coffee into a small bowl with a pouring lip. Sprinkle the gelatine over the surface and, when it becomes spongy, whisk until smooth.

Pour the mixture back into the saucepan and stir until completely dissolved. Stir in the coffee liqueur, then strain into six coffee cups or small glasses. Allow to cool to room temperature, then cover and refrigerate overnight, or until the jellies have set.

Just before serving, put the cream, icing sugar and vanilla extract in a bowl and lightly whip. Dollop the cream over the jelly and spinkle with cinnamon.

basics

mayonnaise

2 large egg yolks, at room temperature
1 tablespoon lemon juice
1 teaspoon sherry vinegar
1 teaspoon dijon mustard
large pinch of sugar
1/2 teaspoon salt
60 ml (2 fl oz/1/4 cup) fruity light olive oil
125 ml (4 fl oz/1/2 cup) mild-flavoured vegetable
    oil, such as canola or sunflower
freshly ground white pepper, to taste

Makes 200 g (7 oz/1 cup)

Make sure the egg yolks and all other ingredients are at room temperature. Put the egg yolks, lemon juice, vinegar, mustard, sugar and salt in a bowl or blender and mix well. Combine the olive oil and vegetable oil and slowly, drop by drop, add them to the egg yolks, whisking or blending all the while, until the mixture is very thick. Season with a little white pepper. Use immediately, or transfer to a clean airtight glass jar and refrigerate — the mayonnaise should keep for several days.

allioli

6–8 garlic cloves, finely chopped
1/2 teaspoon salt
2 large egg yolks, at room temperature
60 ml (2 fl oz/1/4 cup) fruity light olive oil
125 ml (4 fl oz/1/2 cup) mild-flavoured vegetable
    oil, such as canola or sunflower

Makes 200 g (7 oz/1 cup)

Make sure the egg yolks and all other ingredients are at room temperature. Grind the garlic and salt to a paste using a mortar and pestle. (If you don't have a mortar and pestle, put the garlic and salt on a chopping board and chop and mash with a heavy knife until a paste forms.)

Put the garlic paste in a bowl or blender, add the egg yolks and mix well. Combine the olive oil and vegetable oil and slowly, drop by drop, add them to the egg yolks, whisking or blending all the while, until the mixture is very thick. Use immediately, or transfer to a clean airtight glass jar and refrigerate for up to 2 days.

glossary

almonds Commonly eaten as a salted snack with drinks, almonds are used extensively in Spanish cookery, in both sweet dishes such as *turron* (Spanish nougat), and savoury dishes, where they are often toasted and ground to thicken sauces. Spain's smooth, round marcona almond is highly regarded for its superior flavour.

anis A Spanish liqueur flavoured with aniseed, available sweet (*dulce*) or dry (*seco*).

aniseed Also known as anise or anise seed, these greenish-brown, licorice-flavoured seeds native to the Mediterranean region are used in sweet as well as savoury cooking, and to make anis liqueur.

bacalao Dried, salted cod, highly popular in the Basque region of Spain. Bacalao must be soaked for about 24 hours before use to remove the excess salt, and to rehydrate the fish.

bay leaves Used frequently in Spanish cookery, just one or two of these elongated, oval-shaped, green-grey leaves add a strong, slightly peppery flavour to simmered dishes and sauces. Bay leaves are also used sparingly in sweet dishes. The fresh leaves are a little stronger than the dried variety and should be stored in the refrigerator, where they will keep for up to 1 week.

besan A high-protein, pale yellow flour made by finely grinding chickpeas. Besan has a nutty flavour and makes an excellent batter for deep-frying foods, and is also used for thickening sauces.

broad beans These large, bright-green beans, also known as fava beans, are available frozen, or fresh when in season. Before use, the beans need to be removed from their pods, blanched in boiling water and slipped out of their skins. Dried broad beans can be added to soups and stews.

butifarra A deliciously mild pork sausage popular in the Catalan region of Spain. The spices used for flavouring vary from region to region, and the sausage itself can be fresh or cured. Only fresh butifarra is used in this book.

calasparra rice Grown in the Calasparra region of Spain, this medium-grained, high-quality absorbent white rice is traditionally used to make paella, and so is also known as paella rice. Bomba is one variety of this premium rice. Calasparra rice was the first rice in the world to be granted Denomination of Origin status.

caperberries Caperberries are the fruit of the caper bush, which appear after the flowers. They are usually preserved in brine, and are most often served in the same way as olives.

capers Capers are the small flowers of the caper bush, which are sold preserved in brine or sometimes just salt. They should be rinsed well before use. They have a piquant flavour and are used sparingly in dressings and garnishes. The smaller the caper, the more aromatic and the more expensive they are.

cava A quality Spanish sparkling white wine produced by the bottle fermentation method, Methóde Champenoise. Like French Champagne, it is protected by Denomination of Origin labelling. This refreshing tipple can also be used to make delicate sweet and savoury sauces.

cayenne pepper A fiery, spicy powder made from drying and grinding the small orange-red fruits of several pungent species of the capsicum family, native to the Cayenne region of French Guyana in northern South America. Due to its heat it should be used sparingly. In some countries it is also known as red pepper.

cep (porcini) Italians call them porcini, the French call them cep. These intensely flavoured mushrooms are highly prized and very expensive. They are available fresh, but are mostly sold as dried slices, which are first soaked in water and added to dishes.

chickpeas These round, pale brown or yellow legumes are commonly used in rustic, homestyle cooking. Dried chickpeas require overnight soaking and patient cooking to make them tender, but tinned chickpeas simply need to be rinsed before use. Before cooking, remove the loose skins by rubbing the chickpeas between your hands and rinsing them in water.

chorizo The best known of all Spanish sausages, chorizos are made from pork and pork fat and flavoured with sweet and hot paprika, garlic and black pepper. Some are cured longer than others. Firm, fully cured chorizos are sometimes available and can be eaten like salami, but the chorizo used in this book is slightly softer and requires cooking due to its shorter curing time. Do not mistake it for the fresh, raw, chorizo-type sausage sometimes now available in butchers.

cider vinegar A sharp, slightly sweet vinegar made from apple cider.

cinnamon The highly aromatic inner bark of several laurel trees native to Sri Lanka and the East Indies can be rolled and sold as quills or sticks, or ground into a spice. Cinnamon can be used to flavour both sweet and savoury dishes.

cumin Indigenous to the eastern Mediterranean, these seeds are used whole or ground to flavour savoury dishes and breads. The pungent, slightly nutty flavour is enhanced by dry roasting before use.

dried muscatels Raisin-like, sun-dried muscatel grapes have excellent flavour and are often sold in small bunches still on the vine. They are a beautiful addition to cheese platters, but are also wonderful in cooking. They can be substituted with raisins.

fennel All parts of this versatile plant lend themselves to culinary uses. The large, white bulb has a delicate aniseed flavour, and its thick, crisp layers are very refreshing when added raw to salads, and turn quite sweet when braised or cooked. The feathery fronds at the top of the bulb have a slightly stronger flavour and are used as a herb. The seeds have a mild, nutty aniseed or licorice flavour, and can be used whole or ground in both savoury and sweet dishes.

flat-leaf parsley Also called Italian or continental parsley, flat-leaf parsley is less well known in English-speaking countries than curly parsley. It has flat, dark green leaves with a zigzag edge, similar to coriander (cilantro) leaves but slightly larger. It has a fresher, more peppery flavour than the curly variety and is used in salads, wet dishes and as a garnish.

guindilla chillies These long, moderately hot Spanish chillies are picked while still green. They have a superb flavour and are most commonly sold preserved in vinegar. Ripe red guindilla chillies are also available, and are often sold dried.

hake A mild-flavoured, large-flaked, white-fleshed fish very popular with Spanish cooks, who call it *merluza*. Blue-eye cod or another large-flaked, white fish can be used instead.

jamón This superb Spanish ham resembles prosciutto, and is used in much the same way. It varies in flavour and texture depending on which region it is made in. Jamón Ibérico, from black Iberian pigs, has a wonderful flavour and aroma as the animals are fed mainly on acorns, as well as figs and olives. The ham is salted and air-dried, then matured for about 24 months. Jamón Serrano (mountain ham) comes from the heavily fattened white pigs of the Sierra Nevada region, which are salted and then air-cured for at least 12 months.

licor 43 A popular sweet, bright yellow Spanish liqueur tasting predominantly of orange and vanilla.

lima beans Also commonly known as butterbeans, these large white beans are most commonly available dried and are delicious in soups and stews.

málaga wine An intense raisin-flavoured fortified Spanish wine, generally served as a dessert wine or between meals. Strictly speaking, true Málaga wine is aged in the Andalusian city of the same name, although the term is also widely used to describe wine of that style produced in the Málaga region.

manchego cheese One of Spain's most famous cheeses, now protected by European Denomination of Origin labelling. True Manchego cheese is made only from the whole milk of Manchega sheep reared in the La Mancha region. This semi-firm cheese has a rich yet mellow flavour that deepens with age.

marzipan A sweetened almond paste used in confectionery and desserts.

morcilla Similar to black pudding, this very rich, northern Spanish sausage is made from pig's meat and blood and is often flavoured with onion, garlic, cinnamon and cloves. The sausages are boiled before being hung up to dry, and are then sometimes smoked. They are often added to stews, casseroles and stuffings, or sautéed and crumbled into other dishes such as scrambled eggs.

paprika Small red capsicums (peppers), varying in heat from mild to hot, are dried (and sometimes smoked), then ground to a rusty red powder that adds both flavour and colour to savoury dishes. Paprika is most commonly sold as sweet or mild (*dulce*), medium hot (*agridulce*) and hot (*picante*). Smoked paprika is also popular in certain regions of Spain and a small amount adds a distinctive smoky flavour to savoury foods.

pimientos del piquillo Small, sweet and slightly hot red capsicums (peppers) which have been roasted and charred, then peeled and preserved in olive oil. Sold in tins or jars ready for use, whole *pimientos del piquillo* can be stuffed then deep-fried or baked in a sauce, or chopped and added to dishes, or puréed into a sauce or soup.

quince paste A thick, sweet paste made from puréed cooked quince, known in Spanish as *membrillo*. Delicious served with cheeses, or melted into a sauce or glaze for sweet and savoury foods.

saffron The reddish-orange stigma of one species of the crocus flower is the most expensive spice in the world due to its painstaking manner of production. Each flower contains only three stigmas, which are laboriously hand-picked, then dried. It can be sold as whole threads, or ground to a powder. Saffron has a pungent, aromatic flavour and intense colour, so only a little is needed in cooking. Beware of cheap imitations. To help bring out the flavour and colour, lightly toast it, then crumble or soak in warm liquid for a few minutes before use.

sherry First made in Jerez de la Frontera, a town in southern Spain, this fortified wine ranges from very dry to very sweet, and accordingly from pale gold to dark amber. It is often sipped chilled as an aperitif, and used extensively in cooking. The sherries used in this book are fino (very dry), manzanilla (fresh but dry), oloroso (sweet and nutty) and Pedro Ximénez (rich, dark and sweet).

sherry vinegar True sherry vinegar is produced from sherry in the Jerez region of Spain, and can be aged in oak barrels or casks for up to 50 years to refine the flavour. This delicious vinegar is used in vinaigrettes and sauces and drizzled onto Spanish dishes as a condiment.

sidra An alcoholic Spanish apple cider.

white tuna The delicious pale, flaky, mild-flavoured flesh from the albacore tuna is sold packed in olive oil in tins and jars, bearing the Spanish names *atun blanco* or *bonito del norte*.

index